The World of *The Walking Dead*

An accessible introduction to the world of *The Walking Dead*, this book looks across platforms and analytical frameworks to characterize the fictional world of *The Walking Dead* and how its audiences make use of it.

From comics and television to social media, apps, and mobile games, utilizing concepts derived from literary studies, media studies, history, anthropology, and religious studies, Matthew Freeman examines the functions and affordances of new digital platforms. In doing so, he establishes a new transdisciplinary framework for analyzing imaginary worlds across multiple media platforms, bolstering the critical arena of world-building studies by providing a greater array of vocabulary, concepts, and approaches.

The World of The Walking Dead is an engaging exploration of stories, their platforms, and their reception, ideal for students and scholars of world-building, film and TV studies, new media, and everything in-between.

Matthew Freeman is Reader in Multiplatform Media and Co-Director of The Centre for Media Research at Bath Spa University, UK. His research concentrates on cultures of media production across the borders of platforms, cultures, industries, and history, publishing extensively on the cultural histories and industrial workings of transmediality. He has also published on such topics as media branding, convergence cultures, and methodological approaches to media industry studies.

Imaginary Worlds

Each volume in the Imaginary Worlds book series addresses a specific imaginary world, examining it in the light of a variety of approaches, including transmedial studies, world design, narrative, genre, form, content, authorship and reception, and its context within the imaginary world tradition. Each volume covers a historically significant imaginary world (in all its manifestations), and collectively the books in this series will produce an intimate examination of the imaginary world tradition, through the concrete details of the famous and influential worlds that have set the course and changed the direction of subcreation as an activity.

The World of *Mister Rogers' Neighborhood*
Mark J.P. Wolf

The World of *The Walking Dead*
Matthew Freeman

The World of DC Comics
Andrew J. Friedenthal

The World of *The Walking Dead*

Matthew Freeman

Routledge
Taylor & Francis Group
New York London

First published 2019
by Routledge
605 Third Avenue, New York, NY 10017

and by Routledge
2 Park Square, Milton Park, Abingdon, Oxon, OX14 4RN

First issued in paperback 2021

Routledge is an imprint of the Taylor & Francis Group, an informa business

Library of Congress Cataloging-in-Publication Data
A catalog record for this title has been requested

ISBN 13: 978-1-03-209371-0 (pbk)
ISBN 13: 978-1-138-30337-9 (hbk)

Typeset in Times New Roman
by Swales & Willis Ltd, Exeter, Devon, UK

For Georgia x

Contents

Acknowledgments

This book began as something of a summer project, but quickly became important in terms of reigniting my current thinking about imaginary worlds. Specifically, the writing of this book allowed me to rethink what an imaginary world really is, what its less tangible components consist of, how media work to articulate them, the role of audiences in reshaping these less tangible components, and – most importantly – why we all need storyworlds in our lives.

First, a big thanks to Mark J.P. Wolf for his generous support throughout the project. A few of the ideas in this book benefited from being published in other journals whose editors also deserve my thanks. An earlier iteration of Chapter 2 was published as '"We don't get to stay the same way we started": *The Walking Dead*, Augmented Television, and Sociological Character-building' in *Frontiers of Narrative Studies* 5:2 (2019). I therefore thank journal guest editors Jan-Noël Thon and Lukas Wilde for their thoughtful suggestions.

As ever, I would like to thank my amazing wife, Carley, for supporting me in my writing endeavors. And also thanks must go to my little girl, Georgia. I began researching this book just as Georgia was welcomed into the world; countless nights were spent with her fast asleep on my chest as I binged my way through *The Walking Dead* on Blu-Ray.

Introduction

Beyond Literary and Media World-building

'I know this sounds insane, but this is an insane world.' Said declaration, championed by Rick Grimes (Andrew Lincoln) around the start of the sixth season of *The Walking Dead*, comes at a point in the apocalyptic zombie drama where the surviving characters are faced with a key dilemma: either stand together and attempt to rebuild some form of civilization, or give in to despair and let the plague of infected zombies feast on those who remain. On the surface, *The Walking Dead* is essentially a tale of world-building. Academic attempts to theorize the concept of building imaginary worlds have been rife in recent years (see, for example, Wolf, 2012, 2016, 2018; Saler, 2012; Anderson, 2015; Boni, 2017), but rarely has the concept of world-building been so intrinsically embedded into the narrative fabric of a fictional world as it is in *The Walking Dead*, a world whose story quite literally hinges on the rebuilding of its world from the ground up. *The Walking Dead* is the tale of a group of survivors who, following the aftermath of an unexplained zombie apocalypse, must work together not only to survive but to create a new world order with new social structures, new values, new modes of communication, and entirely new ways of living. Still, there is a case to be made that the world of *The Walking Dead* – across all its media – becomes a worse place as time goes on: as seasons on television increase and as issues of comic books mount up, the fictional world on display often becomes filled with less and less hope for the future. Even the main *Walking Dead* logo seen during the opening credits of the television series has been subtly decaying season by season to reflect the increasing decay of the imaginary world.

Not necessarily a story of world-*building*, then; *The Walking Dead* is just as much about the fragmentation of its fictional milieu. Characters roam between desolate locations in the hope of finding somewhere – anywhere – that might one day resemble the world they once knew. *The Walking Dead* is about searching the remains of an imaginary world, a world of empty spaces and violent creatures. And this theme of searching is important, since the way in which one goes about conceptualizing an imaginary world shapes the frameworks and perspectives through which it is made sense of. For instance, approaching *The Walking Dead* through the lens of world-creation might lead one to explore critical lenses drawn from the likes of literary studies or media studies. But it seems equally reasonable that understanding depictions of a fictional world's fragmentation – the downturn of its societal structures, the loss of its characters' moral values, the absence of represented technologies, for example – is something that approaches from philosophy, anthropology, and certainly history could help us with. Which brings me to this book's first overarching objective. Imaginary worlds are perhaps the most innately interdisciplinary of media constructs, encompassing as they do dynamics of fictional cultures, peoples, histories, politics, places, spaces, and so on, and yet ironically few have attempted to analyze explicitly how different disciplinary approaches can yield greater understandings of imaginary world phenomena. This book aims to do precisely that, to make a deliberately transdisciplinary contribution to the study of world-building. It looks across different disciplinary perspectives, in turn expanding the critical toolkit via which imaginary worlds are analyzed by developing a new transdisciplinary framework.

Specifically, I will interrogate the value of a number of different disciplinary concepts and perspectives in enabling us to understand and characterize the fictional world of *The Walking Dead* across media. While the figure of the zombie is ubiquitous in popular culture – spanning everything from cinema to 'popular literature and comic books to video games and smartphone applications' (Christie and Lauro, 2011: 1) – this is not another book about the prominence of the zombie across popular media (see Gagne, 1987; Paffenroth, 2006; Bishop, 2010; Wetmore, 2011). Instead, while serving as an accessible introduction to the world of *The Walking Dead*, this book takes a transmedia approach to examining this imaginary world *beyond* its zombies – utilizing concepts derived from different corners of literary studies, media studies, history, anthropology, religious studies, and philosophy – while looking across comic books, television, social media, apps, and mobile games. Which brings me to the book's second overarching objective: the world of *The Walking Dead* is arguably at the forefront of how emerging digital media technologies are now being used as world-building apparatus. The platforms of many of its extensions are constructed via innovative uses of things like augmented reality (AR), mobile gaming platforms, and social media channels, each of which afford unique interactive opportunities to build storyworlds. While these various digital platforms have certainly not escaped the clutches of academics, far less attention has been paid to what the technological affordances of each of these platforms mean to ideas of world-building.

This combined transdisciplinary and transmedia approach will enable me to assess how the pieces of this particular imaginary world fit together (or contradict each other), which ones presuppose each other, which ones are self-sufficient and which ones are not, and which patterns of use dominate. Building on Mark J.P. Wolf's understanding of imaginary worlds as complex and layered experiential phenomena, this book uses the world of *The Walking Dead* to exemplify a new way of analyzing world-building that goes beyond media-based approaches, proposing a new transdisciplinary framework for analyzing imaginary worlds. The book engages directly in technologies of production, dissemination, and consumption, i.e. the particular technologies utilized in the construction and distribution of narrative texts, and the technologies by which media audiences consume them, in order to ascertain, across different media, the specific ways by which a particular media platform or digital technology distinctly informs the creation of the world of *The Walking Dead.*

And this focus is significant for our purposes, for the world of *The Walking Dead* – perhaps one of the most widely known and popular imaginary worlds of the past decade – is one that is built up via an experiential and emotional bleeding of the line between the analogue and the digital. While such a collision of old and new media has been extensively theorized as the lynchpin of contemporary media convergence (Jenkins, 2006) and its related transmedial practices (see Evans, 2011; Holt and Sanson, 2014), few have considered what these technological 'collisions' mean to practices of world-building and world-consumption specifically. Due to the multiplicity of ways via which imaginary worlds are now engaged with across so many potential media forms, achieving this aim means studying imaginary worlds via a broader arsenal of conceptual tools taken from far more social, historical, and anthropological disciplinary approaches, yielding it is does a more holistic and culturalized understanding of how a given imaginary world becomes embedded in the everyday lives of its audiences and shaped by a range of real-world phenomena. Lubomír Doležel (2010) once stated that you cannot truly interpret a fictional world without grounding it to terms and concepts found in the real world. As Frank Branch and Rebekah Phillips (2018: 383) also observe in this vein: 'A well-structured ontology becomes an encyclopedia that grounds frames of reference within a transmedia fictional world to the world we live in. This grounding allows a scholar to traverse these worlds using a common theory of existence.'

So, through the lens of *The Walking Dead*, this book assesses what we can learn about world-building dynamics by making better use of theoretical approaches and concepts from different corners of academic disciplines, and how such a transdisciplinary approach can be mapped to the affordances of emerging digital technologies on shaping imaginary worlds. But a key question still remains: why study the world of *The Walking Dead* specifically? The answer to this question is simple: *The Walking Dead* is arguably one of the most popular and well-known imaginary worlds of the past decade; as hinted above, its approach to transmedia world-building – making use of all kinds of digital technologies in innovative and forward-thinking ways – opens up new ways of thinking about and analyzing imaginary worlds. But as Elizabeth Evans (2015) notes, 'transmedia strategies operate not just at the level of the text; it is also happening at the level of the *channel* or at the level of the broadcaster themselves.' AMC, home of the world of *The Walking Dead*, is a leading cable and network channel that is committed to pushing forward the means by which the storyworlds of its programs are extended across multiple media platforms. After all, as of 2013 its official slogan has been 'Something More,' a statement of intent to 'construct different story forms that are bound together by an overarching single transmedia estate – guided by a channel or broadcaster's brand identity' (Evans, 2015). As AMC's Vice-President Linda Schupack explained of the rebranded slogan: 'AMC: Something More speaks to our promise to viewers to provide an experience that is unexpected, unconventional and uncompromising. However we express the brand, we want to give our audience something deeper, something richer, *something more*' (Goldberg, 2013). In effect, AMC exemplifies the kinds of cutting-edge developments in transmediality and world-extension strategies that operate across today's media industries.

Written by Robert Kirkman with art by Charlie Adlard and Tony Moore, *The Walking Dead* comic book series was first published by Image Comics in 2003 and, at the time of writing, has reached issue 177 with no immediate end in sight. Outside of the 'big two' comic book publishers – that is, DC and Marvel – *The Walking Dead* is consistently one of the biggest-selling graphic serials. 2012's milestone issue #100 was the number one comic of the year by a significant margin (Berriman, 2013: 9), while 2017's #163 was the highest-ordered comic in close to 20 years (Salazar, 2017). But aside from its mass popularity, there is also a degree of prestige associated with *The Walking Dead* comic book. In 2010, it received an Eisner Award – the comic equivalent of the Oscar – for best continuing series.

The story of *The Walking Dead* (both comic book series and later AMC-produced television series, itself debuting on October 31, 2010) follows Sheriff Rick Grimes who, in the opening scene, is hospitalized following a violent shoot-out. Upon waking from a coma, Rick finds the hospital deserted, at least by the living: mutilated corpses line the hallways and 'undead' zombies populate the hospital canteen. Not just confined to the hospital, though – these undead zombies have populated the entire world, leaving what is left of the human race to fight for survival in a post-apocalyptic scenario where civilization has largely collapsed.

Following 'its beginnings as a small indie comic, the harrowing tale of survival in a zombie-infested world has grown to become a world-wide multimedia phenomenon' (Berriman, 2013: 9). Alongside a range of digital transmedia extensions, i.e. mobile games, webseries, apps, AR experiences, and so on, which themselves will be the primary focus of this book, the world of *The Walking Dead* has spawned a range of physical board games and merchandise, including action figures, t-shirts, mugs, and so on (see Jewitt, 2013). What's more, a string of novels has been published since 2012, as well as occasional short novels, some of which have appeared inside *The Walking Dead: The Official Magazine*.

As will be argued throughout the pages of this book, *The Walking Dead*'s transmedia world-building is best characterized by various forms of subjectivity; my key contribution lies in examining the ways in which an imaginary world can shape, interlace with, and inspire the daily behaviors, emotions, beliefs, and choices of audiences, demonstrating how the act of engaging with a world across media can transform both the person and the storyworld itself. All of this means that a closer examination of the technologies enabling this kind of world-building to happen is needed, as is my analysis of the world of *The Walking Dead* via more historiographical, sociological, anthropological, religious, and philosophical disciplinary concepts. For now, though, let's explore how the fields of literary studies and media studies have previously been used to interrogate the world-building of *The Walking Dead*, partly to set out some useful concepts and partly to highlight the need to go beyond these concepts.

World-building in Media and Literary Studies

Imaginary worlds have been the preoccupation of media scholars and creators for a long time.

While Dudley Andrew (1984: 54) offers a somewhat vague description of storyworlds, defining them as 'comprehensive systems that comprise all elements that fit together within the same horizon,' Smith (2012: 29) defines the concept of storyworld more precisely as 'the spatio-temporal model of story that a given narrative evokes, and which incorporates sequences of events, the characters who instigate them ... and the settings that contextualise these events and characters.' Put simply, a storyworld is built up of characters, events, and settings – just like any story. For as Marie-Laure Ryan (2013) points out, 'the ability to create a world – or more precisely the ability to inspire the mental representation of a world – is the primary condition for any text to be considered a narrative.' Yet what differentiates a basic storyworld that exists in any story from the process of world-building is the way that the spatio-temporality of a given storyworld becomes expanded across texts and media by using those additional forms to add new aspects of world mythology, or to expand the timeline of the storyworld to include new events, or to explore new fictional settings, and so on. As television producer Tim Kring puts it, world-building is 'like building your Transformer and putting little rocket ships on the side' (Kushner, 2008). Well before *The Lord of the Rings* (1954–1955), for example, J.R.R. Tolkien created thousands of years of fictional history, even naming the world's forests and rivers while developing new languages for the inhabitants of Middle Earth. Across this novel, its appendices, and its predecessor story *The Hobbit* (1937), Tolkien expanded the timeline of the storyworld, narrating earlier or parallel events that occurred in the background or tangentially to the primary story. Such world-building activity was in this case done via both the basic principles of story – character, events, and settings – and also via other paratextual documents, indicating the point that, as Wolf (2012: 68) states, the act of building imaginary worlds is often 'transmedial in nature.'

Media texts do not merely forge stories or characters, then; they build worlds in the service of characters and stories. But that does not explain how imaginary worlds are actually built, nor how particular technologies and social phenomena shape their construction. World-building, according to Henry Jenkins (2006: 335), concerns 'the process of designing a fictional universe . . . that is sufficiently detailed to enable many different stories to emerge but coherent enough so that each story feels like it fits with the others.' For Jenkins (2006: 21), 'to fully experience any fictional storyworld, consumers must assume the role of hunters and gatherers, chasing down bits of the story across media channels . . . to come away with a richer entertainment experience.' In economic terms, then, world-building operates on the basis that audiences will gain a richer and fuller understanding of a given imaginary world by consuming more media texts that narrate adventures from that world (Freeman, 2016).

Elsewhere, indeed, media scholars have attempted to address the question of how the pieces of a given imaginary world might fit together (or perhaps contradict each other) by analyzing the building of imaginary worlds in terms of 'production via industrial paratexts and discourses' (Hills, 2017: 345). Jonathan Gray's concept of the 'paratext,' for instance, refers to those media items that sit in between products and byproducts, between ownership and cultural formation, between content and promotional material. For Gray (2010), the meaning of contemporary media stories is no longer located solely within the main texts themselves (e.g. in films, television episodes), but also extends across multiple platforms such as online materials, promotional additions, toys, and DVDs. These kinds of media paratexts can aid the audience's 'speculative consumption' of a story as 'entryway paratexts' and in turn extend the storyworld by providing new narrative content (Gray, 2010: 25).

That said, the use of paratexts to provide entry points into a storyworld requires some system of coordination that Jason Mittell describes as 'orienting paratexts,' which reside:

> outside the [hyper]diegetic storyworld, providing a perspective for viewers [and readers] to help make sense of a narrative world by looking at it from a distance – although as with all such categorical distinctions, actual practices often muddy such neat dichotomies. Orientation is not necessary to discover the canonical truth of a storyworld but rather it is used to help figure out how the pieces fit together or to prose alternative ways of seeing the story that might not be suggested by or contained within the original narrative design.
>
> (Mittell, 2015: 261–262)

From this perspective, then, world-building occurs not only in the textual storyworld, but also in disparate paratexts, through the delivery of exposition and explication. Viewing these elements as somehow 'outside of the storyworld' is indeed problematic, for 'analyzing world-building narratives is nearly impossible without acknowledging that one of their major constituents is the proliferation of various appendices, additions, expansions, supplements or paratexts' (Maj, 2015: 87). As Gray (2010: 7) puts it, the media texts that comprise an imaginary world are 'a larger unit than any film or show [or comic book, novel, etc.] that may be part of it; it is the entire storyworld as we know it.' Paratextual framings and the blending of so-called 'content' and 'promotion' are thus integral components of world-building, actively forming part of 'the text' of an imaginary world rather than reduced to 'a body of extra-diegetic supplementary commentary' (Csicsery-Ronay Jr, 2012: 502).

However, while extra-diegetic supplementary materials will be examined in this book, such as interview footage and social media posts, the concept of paratext only gets us so far in characterizing world-building. Consider 'Just Another Day at the Office,' a short novel written by Robert Kirkman and Jay Bonansinga and first published inside the debut issue of *The Walking Dead: The Official Magazine* in 2012. The story of this short novel takes place right after the events of *The Walking Dead: Rise of the Governor*, the first of the novel series also written by Kirkman and Bonansinga in 2012. In effect, 'Just Another Day at the Office' is a paratext supporting the comic book series, expanding the storyworld by telling the tale of why the people of Woodbury began to trust the Governor, a character who is seen leading Woodbury when readers of the comic book are first introduced to him. But it is also a paratext within a paratext, since the short novel was published inside *The Official Magazine*. And the magazine – published by Titan Publisher four times a year and featuring behind-the-scenes explorations of the comic book series, the television series, the novels, the games, etc. – acts like an orienting paratext for the world of *The Walking Dead*, but one that cannot really disguise the fact that the different media artifacts of the storyworld do not always function in tandem. As William Proctor (2014: 8) puts it, '*The Walking Dead*'s transmedia world-building is both continuous and, at times, discontinuous.' The story of the television series has veered away from that of the comic book; different media feature different events with new characters and story arcs, some of which carry over and extend from other media, while others do not. '*The Walking Dead* is *The Walking Dead*,' explains Jake Rodin – a designer on the soon-to-be-analyzed Telltale Games series – but the point is that some paratexts are in line with the style of the comic books, others adhere to the continuity of the television series, while others are shaped by both, extending and enhancing the storyworld of *The Walking Dead* through transmedia operations (Jarratt, 2013: 102). For as Rodin further implies, '[the game] is from the comic book world but it's similar to the TV show . . . . The comic is sort of the hub and the TV series is a spoke off of that and we're another spoke' (Jarratt, 2013: 103).

The idea of the world of *The Walking Dead* being 'spokes on a wheel' with the comic book as 'center' or, as the above statement posits, 'hub,' with other media artifacts connected via alternate spokes that may or not function in tandem, highlights the limits of analyzing this imaginary world through the lens of paratext. While all of the media artifacts may share *The Walking Dead* brand, the complexity surrounding the industrial logics of each of these media artifacts means that is often unclear which 'spoke' of the storyworld a given set of paratexts belongs to, which is then complicated further as paratexts circulate more widely digitally.

Thus, in an attempt to theorize different modes via which branded paratexts can circulate in the contemporary digital media landscape, Henry Jenkins (2011) identifies two binary approaches to how fictional storyworlds tend to be extended across multiple media – neither of which exemplify the world of *The Walking Dead*. The first approach places ample emphasis on world *continuity*, where 'all of the pieces have to cohere into a consistent narrative world.' The second model, meanwhile, 'celebrates the *multiplicity* which emerges from seeing multiple versions of the same stories unfold' (Jenkins, 2011). By way of example, the Marvel Cinematic Universe would certainly demonstrate the former model – where all of the various stories and their characters intertwine within a single transmedia storyworld – while the DC Extended Universe produced by Warner Bros and DC Comics showcases the latter, where audiences are exposed to multiple, contradictory versions of Batman in film and on television, a strategy which altogether works to engage different audiences in diverse ways.

On the surface, the world of *The Walking Dead* may seem to fit Jenkins' multiplicity model of transmedia world-building – presenting an alternate, televisual version of largely the same stories unfolding in comics. However, to reiterate the above characterization, the world of *The Walking Dead* is more akin to 'spokes on a wheel,' some of which function in tandem and some of which do not. While Jenkins' binary conception of continuity versus multiplicity is certainly characteristic of many of the transmedia storyworlds that now pervade today's popular culture, in the case of the world of *The Walking Dead*, at least, it is perhaps less useful to discuss 'one world' – or even 'multiple worlds' – and instead more appropriate to consider the function of the philosophical and literary studies concept of 'possible worlds.'

So, looking beyond media studies and towards the field of literary studies, the latter field has been instrumental in theorizing the concept of the imaginary world in ways that may be helpful to our initial understanding of the world of *The Walking Dead*. The concept of 'possible worlds theory,' indeed originally introduced in philosophical logic and since borrowed for understanding fictionality in literary theory, stems primarily from work by Marie-Laure Ryan (1984, 1991, 2005), Lubomír

Doležel (1988), and Thomas Pavel (1986). In narratological terms, Ryan (2005) points to the value of possible worlds theory in assessing the structure and ontology of imaginary worlds. In short, in literary studies, possible worlds theory refers to the *simultaneity of imaginary worlds*; the theory accounts for the way that two or more fictional realities, perceptions, and objects can co-exist in the same space-time within a given fictional realm, albeit – and here is the deal-breaker – in ways that suggest a 'contrast between the actual and the possible' (Ryan, 2005: 488). Taking into account Jarratt's prior description of the world of *The Walking Dead* as a series of proverbial 'spokes' that shoot off from one another, possible worlds theory thus fails to make sense of this particular world: possible worlds implies a divide between actuality and mere possibility, whereas *The Walking Dead* presents multiple realities not as possibilities but objectively.

By way of example, and to elaborate on my above observations, *The Walking Dead* is split murkily across two parallel iterations: there are two different series of action figures, one based on the comic book series and one on the television series. There are also two different *Walking Dead* board games – again, one a television version and the other a comic book version. Some transmedia extensions, such as the previously mentioned novels including *Rise of the Governor* and *The Road to Woodbury*, both published in 2012, act as parallel narratives to the comic book series; meanwhile, other transmedia extensions, such as the soon-to-be-examined webseries and social media content, extend and enhance the television series. Analyzing the world of *The Walking Dead* via the literary approach of possible worlds theory may not allow us to understand how the pieces of this world fit together across media, then, but it does at least enable us to think of imaginary worlds less as binaries, i.e. between continuity and multiplicity models, and more as complex ontological spaces that are at once self-sufficient and unified, branching off a new 'spoke' where new stories become possible.

And yet one of the key conceptual ways via which imaginary worlds have been analyzed is via notions of consistency, referring to 'the degree to which world details are plausible, feasible, and without contradictions' (Wolf, 2012: 43). Consistency has been central to understandings of the ontological make-up of imaginary worlds for a while, and Rodrigo Lessa and João Araújo (2018: 90) illustrate this fact via reference to the Leibnizian philosophy concept of compossibility, which concerns 'the logical premise that for a set of entities to be able to coexist in the same world, they must not be mutually contradictory; that is, they must be possible in conjunction (compossible)' (Leibniz, 1989: 661–662).

However, Matt Hills (2017: 344) argues that some scholars are too quick to assume that world-building equates to consistency (or compossibility), pointing out that objects which may contradict a given set of implicit world rules can in fact be 'a significant factor in extending hyperdiegetic worlds.' According to Hills (2017: 344), in fact, this adoption of world-building 'discontinuity' does not mean 'iterating more of the same – or simply adding to a stockpile of narrative facts or lists' – but rather means giving audiences 'unexpected variations on familiar narratives.' Hills may be talking about internal narrative discrepancies, specifically in the 'Whoniverse,' but his point about moving away from analyses of textual world-coherence within transmedia worlds is relevant to the aims of this book – not least of all because transmedia worlds are, by definition, shaped by very different technologies.

The resistance to move beyond the single medium and across a broader array of technologies is arguably one of the limitations of analyzing imaginary worlds via literary perspectives. For instance, according to Ryan (2014), all imaginary worlds consist of six components: *existents*, i.e. the characters and the objects that have special significance for the plot; *settings*, i.e. the space in which the existents are located; *physical laws*, i.e. the principles that determine what can and cannot happen in the world; *social rules and values*, i.e. principles that determine the obligations of the characters; *events*, i.e. the causes of the changes that happen in the time span of the narrative; and *mental events*, i.e. how the individual characters react to both actual and perceived events. From a literacy perspective these six components are solid – and in fact they will be used to structure my own analysis – but more work is needed to understand how these world-building principles work in the context of transmedia worlds, not to mention more interactive media forms like apps and mobile games, or immersive media forms like AR, or participatory forms like social media.

For as has been hinted already, there is a degree of messiness to the world of *The Walking Dead*; its status as an imaginary world thus cannot be fully understood via literary and media studies concepts such as paratext or possible worlds theory. Work in these fields concludes that *The Walking Dead* world is akin to 'spokes on a wheel,' and thus its paratextual structures do not join up in compossible terms, nor does this imaginary world fit neatly into one of Jenkins' models. It is not, however, that the world of *The Walking Dead* – or, for that matter, any equivalent storyworld now pervading popular culture – fails to 'join up' in world-building terms; rather, it is simply that a multiplicity of other disciplinary approaches is needed in order to make sense of this particular imaginary world in world-building terms. For as Ryan (2016: 13) puts it, 'a storyworld is not just the spatial setting where a story takes place; it is a complex spatio-temporal totality that undergoes global changes.' Far beyond the world of *The Walking Dead*, as media scholars we need to broaden our world-building toolkit by looking to other disciplines, and indeed to better assess how a range of different disciplinary concepts work with specific technological affordances to determine storyworld dynamics.

A Transmedia Experience Approach

In some respects, embracing the messiness of a multiplicity of disciplinary perspectives is precisely what transmedia studies is now doing, focusing on experiential digital technologies. Thinking in experiential and real-world terms is indeed nothing if not timely given the way in which understandings of transmediality – itself a larger umbrella conception through which imaginary worlds are typically framed on account of their 'transnarrative, transauthorial and transmedial nature' (Wolf, 2012: 68) – are quite similarly shifting towards notions of audience experience and the social dynamics and possibilities of transmedia practices. Taking a transmedia approach to my analysis of the world of *The Walking Dead* makes sense for all kinds of reasons. First, as both Jenkins (2006) and Evans (2011) have pointed out elsewhere, the principle of world-building is inherent to the logic of transmediality, which Evans (2011: 1) defines most broadly as 'the increasingly popular industrial practice of using multiple media technologies to present information concerning a single fictional world through a range of textual forms.' As a practice, transmediality has become one of the dominant ways by which the flow of entertainment across media is now understood, and is closely associated with what Benjamin Birkinbine, Rodrigo Gómez, and Janet Wasko (2017: 15) refer to as the global media giants – 'the huge media conglomerates such as Disney and Time-Warner, [which] take advantage of globalization to expand abroad and diversify' across media.

But taking a transmedia approach makes sense for another reason, too. Transmediality has equally gained wider relevance as emerging digital screen technologies have multiplied, with the so-called 'old media' of film and television now experienced through online transmedia distribution practices (Evans, 2015), whereby content becomes integrated with social media, companion apps, and other online platforms. Part of this book's aim is to better understand how these kinds of online digital technologies shape world-building dynamics, enabling audiences to go both 'into-the-scenes' and 'behind-the-scenes' of an imaginary storyworld while granting online practices of curation, aggregation, and collaboration.

And yet there is an even stronger reason for taking a transmedia approach. Much like this book's attempt to analyze explicitly how different disciplinary approaches can yield greater understandings of imaginary world-building, let's not forget that transmediality has been defined through very different disciplinary lenses, be it in terms of storytelling (Jenkins, 2006; Evans, 2011; Ryan, 2013), marketing (Gray, 2010; Grainge and Johnson, 2015), journalism (Gambarato and Alzamora, 2018), world-building (Wolf, 2012); historical culture (Freeman, 2016), activism (Scolari, Bertetti, and Freeman, 2014), literacy (Scolari, 2016), and so on. Even more recently, Gambarato (2018) and I revisited uses and meanings of transmediality across different industries, arts, cultures, and practices, noting that there is a consistent and clear emphasis on understanding transmediality as *experience via technology*, offering a somewhat revised definition of the art of transmediality as that which 'builds experiences across and between the borders where multiple media platforms coalesce – experiences that thrive on connecting, sharing, and responding' (Freeman and Gambarato, 2018: 6). We also sought to push the sub-field of transmedia studies towards describing different configurations that transmediality might take in different contexts and platforms.

In terms of studying the artistry of transmediality, in other words, it is important that we return, somewhat contradictorily, to a *medium-specific approach* to studying individual platforms in order to better understand the role that specific platforms play in and across the (trans)media landscape. There is a danger that comes with describing the convergences of contemporary media – namely, that convergence becomes directly associated with blending all forms of different media together into single sites of digital media artifacts. For even amidst a time of apparent technological convergence, mobile and online media, second screening, and so on, it is crucial to remember that different media still operate with largely specific sets of affordances, practices, policies, and consumption habits (Smith, 2018). Thus in order to understand the world-building transmedia potentials of comparatively new media platforms, such as AR, for example, we first need to understand what AR – as an individual platform with distinct affordances – can actually *do*.

Hills (2018: 224), too, has called for the 'need to consider transmedia not just as storytelling but also as a kind of experience,' noting: 'Given that transmedia extensions occur within a proliferating, ubiquitous screen culture, the issue of transmedia's locatedness in space and place has generally been under-explored' (2018: 224). While Hills is referring specifically to set tours, immersive theatrical plays, and walkthrough experiences, my own approach to the term 'transmedia experience' is less to do with ideas of 'being there' (Hills, 2017: 245) and more about the multifaceted, multi-perspectival ways via which the use of different digital media across a multitude of screens, technologies, and locations works in different ways to engage audiences in a highly experiential and personalized manner. As will be seen throughout this book, subjectivity can be key to how audiences engage with and experience an imaginary world; a transmedia experience may actively encourage audiences to question their own subjective experience of a storyworld. Conceptualizing transmediality as experience via technology – studying both 'the techno-social development of digital media and the sociocultural development of fan studies' (Boothe, 2018: 61) – provides a useful approach for making sense of the world of *The Walking Dead*, emphasizing ultimately what Boothe describes as an 'intra-textual' framework for analyzing how 'interactive elements' and 'the influence of fans' is held together within a transmedia network (Boothe, 2018: 67).

Methodologically, moreover, this emphasis on studying experience via technology also justifies my focus on certain media platforms only. Given that *The Walking Dead* comic books were the inauguration of this imaginary world, operating as the core text on which everything else it built, it is crucial to begin this book with the comics. But beyond the start of the first chapter, this book focuses on the building of imaginary worlds via *screen media*, looking in particular at immersive and interactive digital media technologies. I therefore do not examine the aforementioned novels, nor the growing number of theme park attractions. Throughout all four chapters I make use of a range of primary research materials, such as an online survey that was completed with around 200 *Walking Dead* fans, itself conducted via *Walking Dead* fan sites and forums, as well as completing textual and discourse analysis of both the *Walking Dead* media texts and the online paratexts relevant to the platform in question.

The Structure of the Book

In terms of chapter structure, the book is divided into four chapters. Taking my lead from Ryan and her earlier outlined six components of imaginary worlds, each chapter will examine how a different set of technologies work to shape one of these six components (with two chapters delving into a couple of these components), exploring particular world-creation processes and dynamics in different *Walking Dead* texts via different disciplinary lenses. Each chapter thus takes a largely medium- and disciplinary-specific approach, with each chapter examining three media artifacts belonging to the larger world of *The Walking Dead*.

Chapter 1 looks at the 'motherships' the *Walking Dead* world: the comic book series, the main television series, and its companion television series *Fear the Walking Dead*. In aiming to make sense of the so-called 'comic-verse' and the 'show-verse,' exploring new ways of thinking about how these two self-sufficient pieces of *The Walking Dead* universe operate together, this chapter demonstrates the value of adopting a historiographical approach to the study of imaginary worlds, drawing on debates from history, philosophy, and literary criticism to explore how this world's portrayal of history shapes its world-building.

Chapter 2 pushes discussions further towards the role of audiences while, as with Chapters 3 and 4, beginning to explore how world-building is shaped by uses and affordances of distinct digital platforms. This chapter identifies the world-building strategies that have been employed in augmenting the televisual experience of *The Walking Dead*, focusing on Internet content including a webisode series, an accompanying talk show, and an app feature. In doing so, I demonstrate how these particular forms of what I call 'augmented television' draw on sociological and anthropological notions of communication, modern social life, and environment in ways that present rich opportunities for sociological world-building.

Chapter 3 explores the world-building strategies that have been employed in and across *The Walking Dead*'s social media platforms. In attempting to move beyond a view of social media as a mere complement to television, this chapter will instead explore how the affordances of three social media platforms – Facebook, Twitter, and Instagram – work to produce distinct world-building contributions. I argue that social media channels present unique opportunities for religious world-building, creating a set of ideas which act as a kind of belief system for fans of the imaginary world that become, in themselves, a kind of faith.

Chapter 4 continues the pattern of Chapters 2 and 3 by exploring, this time, the world-building strategies that have been employed in and across a range of *Walking Dead* mobile gaming platforms, looking across different kinds of devices and technologies. I argue that interactive mobile-based technologies present new opportunities for philosophical world-building on account of the degree of moral choice and ontological ambiguity that these kinds of technologies afford, offering users interactive philosophical experiences whose moral choices are given greater weight on account of their perceived proximity to the real world.

Finally, the conclusion pulls together all of the themes and lessons learned from the previous four chapters and aims to establish a new transdisciplinary framework for analyzing imaginary worlds across multiple media, bolstering the critical arena of world-building studies by providing a greater array of vocabulary, concepts, and approaches.

References

Anderson, Kevin J. 2015. *Worldbuilding: From Small Towns to Entire Universes*. New York: WordFire Press.

Andrew, Dudley. 1984. *Concepts in Film Theory*. Oxford: Oxford University Press.

Berriman, Ian. 2013. *The SFX Book of The Walking Dead*, vol. 1. London: Future Publishers.

Birkinbine, Benjamin, Gómez, Rodrigo, and Wasko, Janet (eds.) 2017. *Global Media Giants*. London: Routledge.

Bishop, Kyle W. 2010. *American Zombie Gothic: The Rise and Fall (and Rise) of the Walking Dead in Popular Culture*. London: McFarland & Company.

Boni, Marta (ed.) 2017. *World Building: Transmedia, Fans, Industries*. Amsterdam: Amsterdam University Press.

Boothe, Paul. 2018. 'Audience and Fan Studies: Technological Communities and Their Influences on Narrative Ecosystems,' in *Reading Contemporary Serial Television Universes: A Narrative Ecosystem Framework*, edited by Paola Brembilla and Ilaria A. De Pascalis, pp. 57–73. London: Routledge.

Branch, Frank and Phillips, Rebekah. 2018. 'An Ontological Approach to Transmedia Worlds,' in *The Routledge Companion to Transmedia Studies*, edited by Matthew Freeman and Renira Rampazzo Gambarato, pp. 383–391. London: Routledge.

Christie, Deborah and Lauro, Juliet (eds.) 2011. *Better Off Dead: The Evolution of the Zombie as Post-human*. New York: Fordham University Press.

Csicsery-Ronay Jr, Istvan. 2012. 'Of Enigmas and Xenoencyclopedia,' *Science Fiction Studies* 39: 500–511.

Doležel, Lubomír. 1988. 'Mimesis and Possible Worlds,' *Poetics Today* 9(3): 475–495.

Doležel, Lubomír. 2010. *Possible Worlds of Fiction and History: The Postmodern Stage*. Baltimore, MD: Johns Hopkins University Press.

Evans, Elizabeth. 2011. *Transmedia Television: Audiences, New Media and Daily Life*. London: Routledge.

Evans, Elizabeth. 2015. 'Building Digital Estates: Transmedia Television in Industry and Daily Life,' paper presented at the *ECREA TV in the Age of Transnationalisation and Transmediation Conference*, Roehampton University, June 22, 2015.

Freeman, Matthew. 2016. *Historicising Transmedia Storytelling: Early Twentieth-Century Transmedia Story Worlds*. London: Routledge.

Freeman, Matthew and Gambarato, Renira Rampazzo. 2018. *The Routledge Companion to Transmedia Studies*. London: Routledge.

Gagne, Paul R. 1987. *The Zombies That Ate Pittsburg: The Films of George A. Romero*. New York: Dodd, Mead & Company.

Gambarato, Renira Rampazzo and Alzamora, Geane C. (eds.) 2018. *Exploring Transmedia Journalism in the Digital Age*. Hershey, PA: IGI Global.

Goldberg, Lesley. 2013. 'AMC Rebrands With New Logo, Tagline,' *The Hollywood Reporter* (13 April). www.hollywoodreporter.com/live-feed/amc-rebrands-new-logo-tagline-431997 (accessed August 14, 2018).

Grainge, Paul and Johnson, Catherine. 2015. *Promotional Screen Industries*. London: Routledge.

Gray, Jonathan. 2010. *Show Sold Separately: Promos, Spoilers, and Other Media Paratexts*. New York: New York University Press.

Hills, Matt. 2017. 'Traversing the "Whoniverse": Doctor Who's Hyperdiegesis and Transmedia Discontinuity/Diachrony,' in *World Building: Transmedia, Fans, Industries*, edited by Marta Boni, pp. 343–361. Amsterdam: Amsterdam University Press.

Hills, Matt. 2018. 'From Transmedia Storytelling to Transmedia Experience: Star Wars Celebration as Crossover/Hierarchical Space,' in *Star Wars and the History of Transmedia Storytelling*, edited by Sean M. Guynes and Dan Hassler-Forest, pp. 213–224. Amsterdam: Amsterdam University Press.

Holt, Jennifer and Sanson, Kevin. 2014. *Connected Viewing: Selling, Streaming and Sharing Media in the Digital Age*. London: Routledge.

Jarratt, Steve. 2013. 'Playing Dead: The Walking Dead Videogame,' *The SFX Book of The Walking Dead* 1: 102–103.

Jenkins, Henry. 2006. *Convergence Culture: Where Old and New Media Collide*. New York: New York University Press.

Jenkins, Henry. 2011. 'Transmedia 202: Further Reflections,' *Confessions of an Aca-Fan: The Official Weblog of Henry Jenkins* (August 1). http://henryjen kins.org/2011/08/defining_transmedia_further_re.html (accessed November 2, 2012).

Jewitt, Rob. 2013. 'Adapting The Walking Dead for Television: "It's Not About the Zombies",' paper presented at *Adventures in Textuality: Adaptation Studies in the 21st Century*, University of Sunderland, May 5–6, 2013.

Kushner, David. 2008. 'Rebel Alliance: How a Small Band of Sci-Fi Geeks Is Leading Hollywood into a New Era,' *Fast Company* (May). www.fastcom pany.com/798975/rebel-alliance (accessed September 21, 2013).

Leibniz, Gottfried. 1989. *Philosophical Papers and Letters*. Dordrecht: D Reidel.

Lessa, Rodrigo and Araújo, João. 2018. 'World Consistency,' in *The Routledge Companion to Imaginary Worlds*, edited by Mark J.P. Wolf, pp. 90–97. London: Routledge.

Maj, Krzysztof M. 2015. 'Transmedial World-Building in Fictional Narratives,' *Image* 22: 83–96.

Mittell, Jason. 2015. *Complex Television: The Poetics of Contemporary Television Storytelling*. New York: New York University Press.

Paffenroth, Kim. 2006. *Gospel of the Living Dead: George Romero's Visions of Hell on Earth*. Waco, TX: Baylor University Press.

Pavel, Thomas G. 1986. *Fictional Worlds*. Cambridge, MA: Harvard University Press.

Proctor, William. 2014. 'Interrogating *The Walking Dead*: Adaptation, Transmediality, and the Zombie Matrix,' in *Remake Television: Reboot, Re-use, Recycle*, edited by Carlen Lavigne, pp. 5–20. Plymouth: Lexington Books.

Ryan, Marie-Laure. 1984. 'Fiction as a Logical, Ontological, and Illocutionary Issue,' *Style* 18(2): 121–139.

Ryan, Marie-Laure. 1991. *Possible Worlds, Artificial Intelligence and Narrative Theory*. Bloomington, IN: Indiana University Press.

Ryan, Marie-Laure. 2005. 'Possible-Worlds Theory,' in *Routledge Encyclopedia of Narrative Theory*, edited by David Herman, Manfred Jahn, and Marie-Laure Ryan, pp. 446–452. London: Routledge.

Ryan, Marie-Laure. 2013. 'Transmedial Storytelling and Transfictionality,' *Poetics Today* 13(3): 361–388.

Ryan, Marie-Laure. 2014. 'Story/Worlds/Media: Tuning the Instruments of a Media-Conscious Narratology,' in *Storyworlds Across Media: Toward a Media-Conscious Narratology*, edited by Marie-Laure Ryan and Jan-Noël Thon, pp. 25–49. Lincoln: NE: University of Nebraska Press.

Ryan, Marie-Laure. 2016. 'Texts, Worlds, Stories: Narrative Worlds as Cognitive and Ontological Concept,' in *Narrative Theory, Literature and New Media: Narrative Minds and Virtual Worlds*, edited by Maria Hatavara, Matti Hyvarinen, Maria Makela and Frans Mayra, pp. 11–28. New York: Routledge.

Salazar, Kat. 2017. 'The Walking Dead #163 the Highest Ordered Comic in Nearly Two Decades,' *Image Comics* (January 12). https://imagecomics.com/content/view/the-walking-dead-163-the-highest-ordered-comic-in-nearly-two-decades (accessed July 3, 2018).

Saler, Michael. 2012. *As if: Modern Enchantments and the Literary Prehistory of Virtual Reality*. Oxford: Oxford University Press.

Scolari, Carlos A. 2016. 'Transmedia Literacy: Informal Learning Strategies and Media Skills in the New Ecology of Communication,' *Telos* 103: 13–23.

Scolari, Carlos A., Bertetti, Paolo, and Freeman, Matthew. 2014. *Transmedia Archaeology: Storytelling in the Borderlines of Science Fiction, Comics and Pulp Magazines*. Basingstoke: Palgrave Macmillan.

Smith, Anthony N. 2012. 'Media Contexts of Narrative Design: Dimensions of Specificity within Storytelling Industries,' PhD dissertation, University of Nottingham.

Smith, Anthony N. 2018. *Storytelling Industries: Narrative Production in the 21st Century*. Basingstoke: Palgrave Macmillan.

Wetmore, Kevin J. 2011. *Back From the Dead: Remakes of the Romero Zombie Films as Markers of Their Times*. London: McFarland & Company.

Wolf, Mark J.P. 2012. *Building Imaginary Worlds: The Theory and History of Subcreation*. London: Routledge.

Wolf, Mark J.P. (ed.) 2016. *Revisiting Imaginary Worlds: A Subcreation Studies Anthology*. London: Routledge.

Wolf, Mark J.P. (ed.) 2018. *The Routledge Companion to Imaginary Worlds*. London: Routledge.

1 Comics and Television
Historiographical World-building

Early in *Fear the Walking Dead*'s second season, Travis (Cliff Curtis), Madison (Kim Dickens), and the rest of their family dock on an island to escape the pursuit of an unknown ship. Investigating a house on the shore, the group meets George (David Warshofsky), a self-confessed amateur anthropologist who recognizes Travis' lineage as Māori. For George, there is an important historic connection between humankind and its land that should not be broken: 'The commitment to keeping family on the same tribal ground so that every life cycle begins and ends on the same sacred earth . . . that's beautiful.' George may be committed to staying on his land during the zombie apocalypse, then, but the series' central protagonists – much like those of its parent series – have resigned themselves to travelling the world for the sake of survival. Interestingly, in both *The Walking Dead* and *Fear the Walking Dead*, it is precisely the removal of tribal ground from a family that enables communities to blend and to thrive, just as characters become almost unrecognizable from their former, civilized selves in order to survive in the new world. Would the once law-abiding Sheriff Rick Grimes, for instance, recognize the single-minded killer he later becomes? The world of *The Walking Dead* is populated with characters who are stripped of their own histories, and that raises questions about the relationship between the different versions of *The Walking Dead* and how this world's portrayal of history shapes this relationship across comics and television.

As stated in the Introduction, the aim of this book is to use the world of *The Walking Dead* as a means of identifying how a range of different disciplinary concepts and approaches associated with 'worlds' in one sense or another, i.e. peoples, societies, cultures, religions, and so on, have been interlaced with digital technologies to shape this storyworld across multiple platforms. But before these digital platforms and technologies are examined later in the book, this first chapter will focus on the 'core' texts of the world of *The Walking Dead*, its 'motherships,' as Jenkins (2009) puts it: the primary media works that anchor the storyworld. As was also noted in the Introduction, I am keen to move beyond the literary and media studies-centric question of adaptation between the media of comics and television. Henry Jenkins (2013) has previously studied the perils and possibilities of *The Walking Dead* as a comics-to-television adaptation, and his analysis echoes common audience-led discourses documented on fan forums indicating that the world of *The Walking Dead* is comprised of separate universes: a 'show-verse' and a 'comic-verse' (DragonRacer, 2016).

However, such a distinction is far too simplistic, as would be the assumption that the world of *The Walking Dead* is about 'unifying as many of [the] previous stories as possible beneath the arch of some *über*-tale' (King, 2004: 685). But it is true that the so-called comic-verse and show-verse are not especially compossible in terms of basic plot and characterization: there have been many characters who have not survived the television series but still exist in the comic book (for example, Carl (Chandler Riggs)), and there are those who died in the comics but have been kept alive in the television series (for example, Carol (Melissa McBride)). Regularly going in new creative directions, the television series has diverged from its comic-based source material in some major ways over the years.

Moving beyond ideas of fidelity and compossibility, however, this chapter takes a historiographical approach to studying these two media. Specifically, I will examine the world-building practices that have been employed in and across *The Walking Dead* comic book series, *The Walking Dead* television series, and the companion television series *Fear the Walking Dead*, exploring how these three series each build the world of *The Walking Dead* by populating it with what Ryan calls 'physical laws' and 'events.' Physical laws refer to the principles that determine what kind of events can and cannot happen in a storyworld, such as animals being able to talk in fairy tales or time travel being possible in science fiction (Ryan, 2014: 35). Events, meanwhile, refer to the events that form the focus of the story (Ryan, 2014: 35). But in order to interrogate how these three series presuppose each other in world-building terms, it is crucial to adopt a complex historiographical approach to studying the world of *The Walking Dead* that draws on a broad range of ideas from an even wider pool of disciplines.

In particular, I will argue that 'polyglossia' – a sociological term referring to the co-existence of multiple languages in one society – becomes a useful metaphor for making sense of the world of *The Walking Dead*, showing how its approach to world-building across the 'relative' terrain of comics and television is akin to 'dialogism,' a historiographical approach derived from narrative theory. Demonstrating the value of historiography in the study of imaginary worlds will thus take us into debates from fields of history, philosophy, and literary criticism. In doing so, I will show how their problematics are relevant to the study of imaginary worlds, at least in the world of *The Walking Dead*. These issues need to be taken into account if the sub-field of imaginary world studies is to develop beyond descriptive mappings into a deeper engagement with notions of audience subjectivity.

Conceptualizing a Historiographical Approach to Imaginary Worlds

Unlike subsequent chapters, which will begin by outlining the key theoretical pillars needed to conceptualize transmedia world-building according to the affordances of their platforms, this chapter will instead use its opening section to establish a way of thinking about a comic book series and its television adaptation not as separate fictional universes but rather as two differing media artifacts that sit together much like two differing recollections of the past. This chapter's focus on the established media of comics and television means that a specific look at the unique affordances of emerging digital technologies and platforms is less needed.

Instead, what is needed here is a clear theorization of how transmedia world-building can be conceptualized as a multi-perspectival process based on historiography and related conceptions from other disciplines based on historical context. This may sound a little vague, so allow me to begin with an example. Long ago, Gotthold Ephraim Lessing, the famous German writer and philosopher, once made the fundamental point that a painting exists in space and all of its parts are perceived simultaneously, whereas narrative exists in time and its parts are perceived sequentially. A painting, Lessing said, even if depicting a scene of some kind, is not in itself narrative, but narrative can be brought to it to give it meaning (Ricoeur, 1984). My reasoning for reciting Lessing's idea is because it hints, albeit indirectly, at the concepts that I will use to interrogate world-building in this chapter. For starters, Lessing helps us to think about historiography and the nature of bringing additional sources to an artifact in order to interpret it; he also therefore hints at the concept of dialogism, which broadly describes how meaning in one source is defined by its relationship to others. Finally, Lessing's example also hints at philosophical ideas to do with polyglossia and relativism, which both – admittedly in different ways – speak of the multiplicity by which meaning may operate in culture according to a particular set of contexts. All of these ideas are useful for making sense of the world of *The Walking Dead*, particularly across comics and television.

So, let's start with the first of these ideas. Put simply, a historiographical approach to analyzing imaginary worlds means, I argue, embracing the plurality of fictional histories – acknowledging that, like history, an imaginary world is comprised of multiple, contradictory perspectives and reports that depend on context. As Gavin Flood (1999: 141) explains: 'Narratives are always historically located . . . necessarily temporal and constrained by the historical circumstances of their occurrence.' Indeed, as Greenblatt (1980) has shown in the context of literature, texts need to be read as interrelated to wider historical narratives and other, parallel fields. Soon I will look at how *The Walking Dead* depicts its own fictional history and draws on historical myths to build its storyworld. But as with the *Walking Dead* comics compared to their televisual counterparts, moreover, historiography would assume that the placing of various sources alongside each other allows them to 'interrogate' each other. In other words, transmedia world-building has much in common with the learning of history. Both the consuming of a transmedia world and the learning of history operates on the basis that people will gain both a richer and fuller understanding of a given story/ event if they consume as many documented fragments relating to it as possible: 'To fully experience any fictional storyworld, consumers must assume the role of hunters and gatherers, chasing down bits of the story across media channels . . . to come away with a richer . . . experience'

(Jenkins, 2006: 21). As such, it is easy to see why a historiographical approach to analyzing transmedia world-building might make sense: if multiple, potentially conflicting histories are embraced, then no one needs to fear that one history will be lost, as will be exemplified via the dialogic relationship between *The Walking Dead* comic books and television series.

Unlike imaginary worlds, however, the learning of history is anything but agreeable; 'it is not a collection of facts deemed to be "official" by scholars on high' (Conway, 2015). Imaginary worlds, by stark contrast – so often 'transnarrative, transmedial, and transauthorial in nature' (Wolf, 2012: 68) – are regularly studied and consumed according to how 'the dispersed pieces of information . . . all fit together to form a meaningful whole' (Jenkins, 2011). Imaginary worlds often operate amongst issues of canon and continuity, with both media producers and fan cultures policing which material is accepted as officially part of the storyworld (Proctor, 2013). Importantly, as Wolf (2012: 46) states, an attempt to 'restor[e] consistency can sometimes equal that of actual historical researchers' establishing facts and revising earlier claims as new data conflicts with them.' But historical research is not always about consistency, nor even can it be, and imaginary worlds – especially those expanded across sequential narratives, such as superhero comics (Reynolds, 1992; Pustz, 1999), television series (Mittell, 2014; Geraghty, 1981), and those that traverse media borders (Jenkins, 2006; Scolari, 2009; Freeman, 2016) – actively encourage dialogical relationships.

The concept of 'dialogism,' theorized by philosopher and literary critic Mikhail Bakhtin (1981), is about discourse and explicitly acknowledges that meaning in one source is defined by its relationship to other instances – both past, to which it responds, and future, whose response it anticipates – thus connecting it to the historiographic approach that is really the core theme of this chapter. Dialogism is the opposite of 'monologism,' itself the refusal of discourse to acknowledge its relational constitution and its misrecognition of itself as independent. How, then, might a dialogic approach to *The Walking Dead* reveal more nuanced ways of discussing its comics and television iterations in world-building terms?

Crucially, Bakhtin's dialogical concept is always embedded within history and context. 'For Bakhtin, the understanding between the "self" and "other" is through historicized, communicative encounter which above all else means through language' (Flood: 1999: 163). Similarly, this chapter will argue against categorizing the so-called comic-verse and the show-verse of *The Walking Dead* as entirely distinct or parallel worlds. Rather, I will argue that these two 'media-verses' exist in a far more complex dialogical relationship that requires ideas and approaches drawn from a range of disciplinary perspectives in order to fully understand it. As we will see, in the case of the world of *The Walking Dead*, at least, the comic book series is acutely *historic* in terms of its relationship with the television series and how it is discursively positioned culturally, with audiences acting much like historiographers insofar as they may choose to piece together their own interpretations of the world's history.

And this idea is really one of 'relativism,' i.e. of making sense of the storyworld in terms of an individual's own personal, social, cultural, technological, and historical context. Relativism, specifically 'truth relativism,' is the doctrine that there are no absolute truths, i.e. that truth is always relative to some particular frame of reference, such as a language or a culture (Baghramian and Carter, 2015). Of central importance to this doctrine is the idea that 'narrative as text pervading culture need not be coherent but can be fragmentary, and the fragmentary nature of texts can serve in turn to create new narratives' (Flood, 1999: 121). In other words, relativism speaks of the multiplicity of narratives that exist in our own lives every day; to most of us, it does not matter how well these narratives 'fit together,' only that we acknowledge their relationship and move forward with our way of seeing that narrative.

Here, we might wish to turn to the Aristotelian narrative distinction between 'the life that is lived' and 'the story that is told.' As Flood (1999: 136) describes it, 'the internalized narratives – the "narrative voices" – which comprise our life provide a sense of identity that constitutes us and is constantly reinterpreted within the contexts of culture.' Such a theory would posit that human beings cannot be the authors, though we can become 'the narrator and the hero of our own story' (Ricoeur, 1984: 32). In other words, media audiences may not be able to be the authors of the world of *The Walking Dead* per se, but they can narrate which version of the world of *The Walking Dead* they choose to believe in. Later I will show how – via audiences surveyed for the purposes of this chapter – the world of *The Walking Dead* is not consumed as any kind of absolute but is rather a reflection of an audience's preferences for particular sets of platforms and their own broader media habits and daily routines.

So, let's now explore these ideas further in relation to some examples and how these concepts inform specific opportunities to populate the world of *The Walking Dead* with physical laws and events. First I will lay out the importance of thinking about the world of *The Walking Dead* as akin to history, before then interrogating the above historiographical ideas, suggesting that an understanding of the relationship between the comic book series and the television series in world-building terms is best characterized through an 'historicized, communicative encounter which above all else means through language' (Flood: 1999: 163).

World as History

The Walking Dead comic books, created by Robert Kirkman and illustrated by Charlie Adlard, are still being produced today. The television series is further behind in the timeline. When it comes to the world depicted in either series, two things stand out: one, that almost nothing is known about the lives of its protagonists before the outbreak, and two, that the very nature of the apocalyptic world on display gives it the feel of being historically located. On a basic level, one might think about how *The Walking Dead* comic books function as the history (as in, the blueprint) of *The Walking Dead* television series, insofar as the former establishes the loose narrative events for the storyworld to which the latter responds. But the relationship between transmedia world-building and history is much more complex than this: history, much like an imaginary world, is not a set narrative; it cannot be easily synthesized into a single, standardized chronicle. As was outlined above, history is made up a 'collection of historians exchanging different, often conflicting analyses . . . students of history would be better served descending into the bog of conflict and learning the many "histories" that compose any given subject' (Conway, 2015). It is worth thinking about the world of *The Walking Dead* in precisely these terms, with the comic books and the television series the different, conflicting analyses. Understanding the past appears to be a universal human need, and the 'telling of history' has emerged independently in civilizations around the world. What constitutes history is a philosophical question, just as it should be for imaginary worlds.

However, before I engage with this historiographical position, first I ask a question: textually, why might it be so prevalent to think about the world of *The Walking Dead* in historical terms? Most obviously, the post-apocalyptic nature of the storyworld lends it a visualized sense of pre-modernization: characters riding on horseback, no technological communication mechanisms, the breakdown of societal structures, and so on. 'The survivors do not live in a new world so much as they live in the decaying body of the old one, the crumbling infrastructure rotting around them like meat falling off the bones' (Hudson, 2014).

Unlike more fantastical worlds, too, this is the kind of storyworld that feels 'real' insofar as it feels historic. Ryan's typology for categorizing imaginary worlds is useful here, which explains how 'imaginary worlds can be situated at variable distances from the world we regard as actual or primary' (2018: 74). Ryan's typology is divided according to 'what could happen in the Primary World [i.e. the real world], given the proper circumstance' and 'what can be imagined but cannot happen in the Primary World' (Ryan, 2018: 74). The first category, based on depictions of what is simply true or false, describes non-fiction; the secondary category, based on depictions of possibility, describes realistic fiction or science fiction; the third category, based on depictions of impossibility, describes fantastic genres. Ryan's logic here is that, for example,

> the world of a realistic novel such as Jonathan Franzen's *Freedom* (2010) stands closer to the actual world than the world of a fantasy such as *The Lord of the Rings* because its description requires fewer modifications from the assumed description of reality than the description of the world of *The Lord of the Rings*.
>
> (Ryan, 2018: 74)

Following this logic, *The Walking Dead* sits murkily across Ryan's second and third categories, since while its fantastical zombies are in no way possible, its focus on what resembles a pre-modernized version of real-world locations like Atlanta in the U.S. is certainly plausible in science fiction.

This idea of the world of *The Walking Dead* being one of quasi-possibility grounded in the reality of the historic is laced into its textual fabric, shaping how it is constructed as a piece of history despite it intentionally not being set in any kind of fictional past. For example, a recurring theme in *The Walking Dead* is the line between dictatorship and democracy. Throughout both the comics and the television series, countless arguments are depicted between characters, mainly over such decisions as where to travel to next, how to get there, who should do what, and how to respond when people break the rules. These arguments are an example of what Ryan calls events, forming the focus of the story. Throughout the course of the narrative, the character of Rick becomes a leader for the group, and at the end of Season 2 on television openly declares a dictatorship over the rest of the survivors: 'This isn't a democracy anymore.' Crucially, the concept of dictatorship has historical connotations, serving as a lens via which the story's events are constructed.

Specifically, the concept of dictatorship originally emerged from Ancient Roman legal convention where an absolute power was bestowed upon an individual in cases of extreme emergency. The Roman dictatorship system was seen at the time as a necessity to protect itself from annihilation by invading armies. The iconography of Roman politics is laced throughout *The Walking Dead*, be it via gladiatorial battles or referenced Bible verses. One could say that Rick is modeled on Cincinnatus, a Roman statesman who was elected by the Roman consul to the position of dictator when Rome was in imminent danger from a neighboring Italian tribe. As legend goes, a group of senators were dispatched to tell Cincinnatus the news and found him plowing his farm. Cincinnatus, having completed his public duty, immediately resigned from his position as dictator. Later, Cincinnatus was elected dictator again, this time to save Rome from a coup. And again, once the coup was stopped, Cincinnatus resigned and went back to farming. Similarly, Rick leaves his new life as a farmer in order to protect his community from a zombie attack only to then go back to farming when the threat is gone. Such comparisons may well be coincidental, but my point is that the world of *The Walking Dead* resembles a moment of pre-modernization much more than it does the twenty-first century, and this resemblance shapes how the storyworld is built.

In turn, this historic iconography shapes how audiences respond to the storyworld, with many – in fact – ascribing a sense of the past when being asked to characterize the world of *The Walking Dead*. For example, one fan – surveyed for the purposes of the book – stated: 'The world of *The Walking Dead* is characterized by a sense of all values held in the world being destroyed – and the survivors trying to come to terms with that.' Another fan simply replied: 'Chaos.' But dig a little deeper and it becomes clear that audiences are describing the storyworld as a regression towards a historical time: 'The structure of everything civilized would be gone with a whoosh, and back in time we go.' As another fan elaborated:

> History sort of goes out the window, and for many groups morals too. The people who we hold up as heroes within *The Walking Dead* are the ones who cling to a culture and history similar to ours [right now], before the turn. The ones who abandon it, we see as villains.

Other surveyed fans, meanwhile, referenced aforementioned ideas of dictatorship in ways that led them to characterizing *The Walking Dead* as a series about our own history:

> There are so many different factions attempting to develop their own societies (Alexandria, the Saviors, the Kingdom, etc.), which are not dissimilar to our history. Alexandria is communism at its purest, with everybody doing a share of the work for the benefit of all; the Saviors are capitalism/dictatorship, with the many working for the benefit of the few, led by a violent, psychopathic dictator; and the Kingdom is a benign dictatorship where the work and its benefits are for all, but the rules and decisions are made by a single man . . . . Much like our own past civilizations in history, some of these 'societies' will rise and fall.

In the case of *The Walking Dead*, then, and to paraphrase Aristotle, there is little difference between 'the story that is told' of our own history and 'the life that is lived' in the storyworld. Furthermore, as stated above, the world of *The Walking Dead* is simultaneously characterized by the way in which almost nothing is known about the lives of its protagonists prior to the outbreak; despite its historic feel, this is an imaginary world that, ironically, has no history. 'It is exceedingly rare,' journalist Alex Mullane (2018) writes, that anyone on *The Walking Dead* ever discusses the world pre-apocalypse.' Indeed, it is notably uncommon in this series to see characters reminisce about their old lives, the things they miss, or the people they lost.

In the past, writers dabbled with some flashbacks to show what characters were like before the outbreak began, but these are few and far between, while no scientific explanation is ever given, in any medium, for what caused the outbreak in the first place. Nothing has been done to bridge the gap between what happened then and what is happening now. Even *Fear the Walking Dead* – set during the onset of the apocalypse – has deliberately avoided answering such questions. The events of the storyworld, in other words, are framed by discrepancy and subjectivity, and as such the impossibility for any single, standardized chronicle of the events of the storyworld. Some audiences may vocalize their frustrations with an imaginary world with so little connective tissue to its own fictional history ('I wish sometimes [the characters] would talk more about what they lost in that regard'), but its 'tribal, animalistic tone,' as another fan described it, keeps the world of *The Walking Dead* firmly entrenched *as*, but not *in*, the past. This semblance of past, combined with the very absence of any objective, authoritative communicative tools in the storyworld itself, lends a historiographic, multi-perspectival approach to world-building, as will be demonstrated next.

World as Historiography

Conceptually, then, transmedia world-building has a great deal in common with the multi-perspectival narratives of a historiographical approach. Let's now explore how *The Walking Dead*'s aforementioned entrenchment as the past shapes the transmedial relationship between the comic book and television iterations in world-building terms, which earlier I suggested is best characterized as an 'historicized, communicative encounter which above all else means through language' (Flood: 1999: 163). So what do I mean by this? Put simply, I mean that, as Conal Furay (1988: 233) observes of historiography more broadly, 'when you study historiography, you do not simply study the events of the past directly,' as per my above analysis of the textual iconography of the world of *The Walking Dead*, 'but also the changing interpretations of those events in the works of individual historians,' or – in our case – audiences. It thus means reiterating the value of dialogism in this particular context, which, as explained previously, acknowledges that meaning in one source (or medium) is defined by its relationship to others: both past, to which it responds, and future, whose response it anticipates. Again, critical to this line of thinking is the idea that 'narrative . . . pervading culture need not be coherent but can be fragmentary, and the fragmentary nature of [multiple] texts can serve in turn to create new narratives' (Flood, 1999: 121).

For example, consider the character of Carol and all of the events that happen to and around her across the media of comic books and television. Carol makes for an intriguing case study because, at first glance, she seemingly exemplifies the need to distinguish the comic-verse and the show-verse as completely separate worlds: the Carol illustrated in the comics is radically different from the one dramatized on screen. In the comic, Carol was killed years ago. Before her death, she was a meek housewife, a much-younger victim of spousal abuse who was entirely dependent on others. In the end, Carol let herself be bitten by a zombie in a demise that was ultimately suicide. By contrast, the Carol of the television series transforms from the would-be home-maker to a pragmatic, utilitarian warrior, at one point saving the entire group from almost certain death in Terminus. As Robert Kirkman explains:

> The Carol that's in the comic was my attempt to show just how broken an individual can become from the zombie apocalypse. The Carol in the show . . . actually is made stronger by all the more horrible things that happen to her in the show.
>
> (Tassi, 2015)

And as per the broader historiographical interest in such conflicting accounts, many of the audiences surveyed for this book, too – each drawn from *Walking Dead* fan sites – expressed a desire to descend into the proverbial bog of narrative conflict and learn the many histories that compose the events of *The Walking Dead*. In theory, one might assume that there are four types of *Walking Dead* fan in the world: one, those who watch the television series but have never read the comics; those who read the comics but have never watched the television series; those who went to the comics after first watching the television series; and those who are comic fans first and watch the television series to see how it will all play out on screen. To some extent these categories might well be true, but what is more significant to note is that nearly 80% of the *Walking Dead* fans surveyed believed that both the comic book and the television series were critical to their experience of the storyworld, with 72% admitting to finding pleasure in the differing, often conflicting narratives unfolding across these two media. 'The multi-platform world of *The Walking Dead* is what I love – we wouldn't want the show to become exactly like the comic,' one fan insisted. 'For me, it is so important that the storylines are not exactly the same – that would be counter-productive to the other media,' another argued. '[The comics and the television series] fit together precisely because they don't – the world always feels the same but the differences are just so fascinating to me.'

By all accounts, the absence of any source of unifying social or technological systems in the world of *The Walking Dead* – as in, the media – deprives the storyworld of the chance to define its physical laws with any degree of certainty or objectivity. Instead, the nature of the storyworld lends itself only to subjective interpretations of events, allowing it to mutate across comics and television. How, then, does *The Walking Dead* build its storyworld without granting it, or its characters, a history? It does so by encouraging a historiographical approach to world-consumption based on the plurality of multiple, often contradictory perspectives that allows fans to act like historiographers, exchanging different, often conflicting analyses. But such an approach also depends on the relativism of context, as will be demonstrated next.

World as Relativism

The aforementioned example of Carol hints at the nature of the world of *The Walking Dead* being one of polyglossia, where – much like multiple languages can co-exist within the same society, each serving different functions – multiple variations of a storyworld can co-exist too, not ontologically, but as a thematic reflection of this world's lack of in-text governance. And hence the world of *The Walking Dead* and its identity across multiple media need not be unitive to function in world-building terms, as Alasdair MacIntyre (1985: 21) might claim, for just as 'there can be many narrative voices within a single life,' so too can there be many narrative divergences and interpretations within a fictional universe; after all, it is made up of multiple characters, each with their own individual perspectives. But if the world of *The Walking Dead* is indeed characterized by its impossibility to form any single, standardized chronicle of its own events and physical laws, then it makes sense to understand the nature of world-building in this particular instance by honing in on the idea of subjectivity as world-building. Or, to put it another way, to approach world-building via the lens of relativism.

As explained above, truth relativism is the doctrine that meaning is relative to a particular context or frame of reference, meaning that – in our case – the physical laws of the *Walking Dead* storyworld are communicated subjectively via an individual character's own personal, social, cultural, or historical context, and audiences, in turn, may interpret those physical laws via their own individual personal, cultural, or technological context. Soon I will elaborate on this latter idea of audiences as enacting relativism, but first let's explore how a prescribed physical law in the world of *The Walking Dead* is itself contingent on relativism.

Consider the physical law of zombie blood and, specifically, its impact on survivors when it comes into contact with human skin. Since the beginning of the world's narrative in both comics and television, there have been numerous instances of characters opting to cover themselves in the blood of zombies in order to disguise their human scent and hide among the undead hordes. During the Season 8 episode 'Dead Or Alive Or' on television, however, Negan (Jeffrey Dean Morgan) proposes a plot to infect Rick by coating his weapons in zombie blood. But during the broadcast of Season 8, some audiences took issue with Negan's plan given various other characters have been seen smothering themselves in zombie blood in the past – with no negative or harmful effect. 'Negan can't think touching blood/guts of the dead will infect people at Hillside!' one Twitter fan protested. 'Haven't Rick et al. spread blood/guts on themselves to safely walk through the dead! Negan himself spread guts on himself!' Or as another fan protested: 'Seasons 1–7 #TheWalkingDead – "rub zombie guts all over you and you can walk among them!" Season 8 of #TheWalkingDead – "that shit will turn you now".' But addressing this discrepancy in the known physical laws of the storyworld as a continuity error fails to recognize the fact that the world of *The Walking Dead* is itself a place without scientific knowledge: there are no media outlets informing citizens of their research into zombies, or no objective, standardized account of what is happening to the world or why. Allan Cameron (2012: 66) points out that the relationship between a lack of knowledge and the media is in fact a convention of the zombie sub-genre more broadly: 'Beginning with George A. Romero's 1968 classic *Night of the Living Dead*, zombie films have . . . focused on the inability of media to communicate the nature, scale, and imminence of the zombie threat.' Cameron (2012: 66) draws attention, for example, to the 'radio and television reports [that] funnel out-of-date information to the embattled survivors in *Night of the Living Dead* and *Dawn of the Dead* (1978), leading them to make fatal misjudgments.' As per the genre trend, then, the world of *The Walking Dead* is plagued by its lack of unifying knowledge: any known understanding of a given physical law is, in other words, *relative*.

For example, characters from the television series, such as Daryl (Norman Reedus), addressed the ambiguity surrounding the effects on zombie blood by admitting, 'sometimes, nothing happens.' As if to confirm the lack of unifying knowledge about zombie blood, *Fear the Walking Dead* – produced by AMC as a 'companion' series to *The Walking Dead* and which debuted on August 23, 2015 – also contributed another relative perspective on the topic, when in Season 4 episode 'Laura' John Dorie (Garret Dillahunt) ferociously stabs a zombie, leaving himself and Naomi (Jenna Elfman) drenched in zombie blood. 'I didn't get bit, it wasn't close enough to bite you,' insists John, to which Naomi snaps back: 'I've seen people get really sick from just being exposed to this stuff.' This serves as another example of world-building as dialogism, with a physical law in the storyworld, i.e. the effect of zombie blood on human survivors, defined not in any singular, canonical sense but only by its relationship to other instances, both past, to which it responds, and future, whose response it anticipates. But it also cements the idea of world-building as relativism, since few absolute truths are known in this world, even about its physical laws. Instead, these laws are known only by a frame of reference, formed by the communities that populate this storyworld.

A clear trajectory is starting to emerge here: the historic representational iconography of the world of *The Walking Dead* informs a kind of historiographical approach to its world-building based on multi-perspectival narratives, and this historiographical approach affords a mode of world-building across multiple, seemingly contradictory media based on relativism. But it does not end here: the impossibility for the world to develop any single, standardized physical laws over fragmentary interpretations based on the relativism of individual context also links to, though does not necessarily inform, the behavioral patterns of audiences in terms of how they consume the storyworld. That is to say that audiences may well *enact* relativism – interpreting the world of *The Walking Dead* via their own technological context.

What, then, do I mean by this? Flood (1999: 137) notes how 'our narratives are always constructed by and within the cultures we inhabit,' just as technologies similarly work to constrain but also afford the ways via which imaginary worlds are built and engaged with. Nearly 80% of the *Walking Dead* fans surveyed may have stressed that both the comic book and the television series were critical to their overall experience of the storyworld, digging into the conflicting narratives unfolding across these two media, but these same audiences also highlighted a striking personal connection to a particular media platform, not because of the narrative or world contribution it makes, but rather because it embodies their own broader media habits and daily routines. Here are some examples: 'The world of *The Walking Dead* is very bitty, nothing exactly ties in, but that's fine as it means I see the world through the eyes I choose,' one fan explained. Another noted: 'The multi-platform content is so important, but everyone has a preferred choice of platform with the franchise. I think it lends itself to that.' What, though, characterizes these patterns of use specifically? 'I personally consume the comic books when I miss the TV series,' one fan commented, while another stated: 'For me, they're both just differing ways into the world – it's like leaving one set of friends or one place to go and meet another. It's a different experience – same, but different.' Interestingly, many audiences explicitly rationalized their personal choice of platforms according to their own media preferences: 'I consume based on what I do anyway. I read the comics, but only as volumes or compendiums because that's how I like to read comics.' Another commented:

I will watch *The Walking Dead* and *Fear the Walking Dead* on TV, because I'm usually in on Sunday nights and I devote that time in front of the TV. But not the games though – they require more involvement and are harder for me to pick up and go with, so I pass on those.

A large cable channel such as AMC may be thinking transmedially so to engage its audiences across multiple platforms, but it is clearly not enough to assume that the creation of a transmedia world is enough to explain the specificities and the reasons for why audiences choose (or choose not) to engage in that world as a transmedial activity. Elsewhere, similarly, I have argued for the need to analyze the behaviors and motivations of a media-crossing audience according to more fluid, ephemeral, and personal reasons, with fans following values, themes, and philosophies (rather than just stories) across multiple media (Freeman and Taylor-Ashfield, 2018). Because of these behaviors, it makes sense that *Walking Dead* audiences would also adopt a kind of historiographical approach to consuming this particular world – not so much interested in hunting and gathering past fictional events that explain the physical laws of the world, but rather in the changing interpretations of those events and physical laws in different media. It is here where the apparent tensions between the world of *The Walking Dead* being one of polyglossia and one of relativism are best exemplified.

Conclusion

The world of *The Walking Dead* may be formed via interconnected digital networks, as will be examined in detail in subsequent chapters. However, the nature of world-building in this case is entirely shaped and – crucially, *reshaped* – by different platforms and technologies, with audiences often understanding this particular imaginary world according to their preference for a particular platform. This demonstrates how audiences may embody ideas of relativism in their media-crossing behaviors and yet, simultaneously, also behave like historiographers in their complex, dialogical engagement patterns with the world of *The Walking Dead*. Such behavioral patterns also work to reinforce AMC's channel brand as that which 'provide[s] an experience that is unexpected, [giving] our audience *something more*' (Goldberg, 2013).

Above all, however, this chapter has shown the importance of the imagination of audiences in terms of the telling of a storyworld, not in any official, standardized canon sense, but rather by way of interpreting and adopting a particular view of a storyworld and allowing that view to shape where they go next in that storyworld. In that sense, it therefore does not matter whether the comic book and television iterations of *The Walking Dead* are compossible or not, because – much like the telling of history – there is no one, standardized chronicle, only ever multiple ways of perceiving the chronicle. Nobody minds that the history books constantly disagree with each other, and nor, it seems, do fans of *The Walking Dead*.

As has been argued throughout this chapter, in history there can be no single official re-telling; historiography is precisely about embracing the idea that hunting down as many (potentially conflicting) versions of history as possible will provide the fullest interpretation. Taking a historiographical approach to the world of *The Walking Dead* – a world that is ideally suited to such a practice given its own textual historic leanings – provides us with a more nuanced and personal way of understanding how two seemingly separate iterations of a storyworld can still function together in world-building terms through the eyes of audiences.

So, where does that leave us? In short, my historiographical approach to analyzing the world of *The Walking Dead*, at least as far as its comic book and television series are concerned, is still predicated on a dialogical relationship between different textual and discursive components of media, but only insofar as this dialogism works as a kind of social organization mechanism for how the different series are perceived. Thus moving away from analyses of 'vast narratives' – where stories become linked under one narrative (Harrigan and Wardrip-Fruin, 2009) – my own historiographical approach has favored multi-perspective narratives in different media that, by deviating and forging new creative paths, allow us to reconcile an imaginary world's past events with its current characterizations. Such an approach lends new ways of thinking about a storyworld's physical laws and events, not as absolutes, but only ever as contexts of relativism in a world defined by contexts of relativism.

References

Baghramian, M. and Carter, J.A. 2015. 'Relativism,' *The Stanford Encyclopedia of Philosophy* (September 11), https://plato.stanford.edu/entries/relativism/ (accessed July 14, 2018).

Bakhtin, Mikhail. 1981. *The Dialogic Imagination: Four Essays*, edited by Michael Holquist. Austin, TX: University of Texas Press.

Cameron, Allan. 2012. 'Zombie Media: Transmission, Reproduction, and the Digital Dead,' *Cinema Journal* 52(1) (Fall): 66–89.

Conway, Michael. 2015. 'The Problem With History Classes,' *The Atlantic* (March 16). www.theatlantic.com/education/archive/2015/03/the-problem-with-history-classes/387823/ (accessed July 2, 2018).

DragonRacer. 2016. *Walking Dead Forums*. April 4. www.walkingdeadforums.com/forum/threads/the-print-comic-is-so-much-different-than-the-tv-show.314801/#post-11674492 (accessed February 19, 2018).

Flood, Gavin. 1999. *Beyond Phenomenology: Rethinking the Study of Religion*. London: Cassell.

Freeman, Matthew. 2016. *Historicising Transmedia Storytelling: Early Twentieth-Century Transmedia Story Worlds*. London: Routledge.

Freeman, Matthew and Taylor-Ashfield, Charlotte. 2018. '"I Read Comics from a Feministic Point of View": Conceptualizing the Transmedia Ethos of the Captain Marvel Fan Community,' *Journal of Fandom Studies* 5(3): 317–335.

Furay, Conal. 1988. *The Methods and Skills of History: A Practical Guide*. Hoboken, NJ: John Wiley & Sons.

Geraghty, Christine. 1981. 'The Continuous Serial: A Definition,' in *Coronation Street*, edited by Richard Dyer, pp. 9–27. London: BFI.

Goldberg, Lesley. 2013. 'AMC Rebrands With New Logo, Tagline,' *The Hollywood Reporter* (April 13). www.hollywoodreporter.com/live-feed/amc-rebrands-new-logo-tagline-431997 (accessed July 14, 2018).

Greenblatt, Stephen. 1980. *Renaissance Self-Fashioning: From More to Shakespeare*. Chicago, IL: University of Chicago Press.

Harrigan, Pat and Wardrip-Fruin, Noah. 2009. *Third Person: Authoring and Exploring Vast Narratives*. Cambridge, MA: MIT Press.

Hudson, Laura. 2014. 'The Walking Dead's Scariest Element Isn't Zombies, It's Memories,' *Wired* (November 2). www.wired.com/2014/02/walking-dead-flashbacks/ (accessed July 13, 2018).

Jenkins, Henry. 2006. *Convergence Culture: Where Old and New Media Collide*. New York: New York University Press.

Jenkins, Henry. 2009. 'The Revenge of the Origami Unicorn: Seven Principles of Transmedia Storytelling,' *Confessions of an Aca-Fan: The Official*

Weblog of Henry Jenkins (December 12). http://henryjenkins.org/2009/12/the_revenge_of_the_origami_uni.html (accessed February 20, 2012).

Jenkins, Henry. 2011. 'Transmedia 202: Further Reflections,' *Confessions of an Aca-Fan: The Official Weblog of Henry Jenkins* (August 1). http://henryjenkins.org/2011/08/defining_transmedia_further_re.html (accessed March 18, 2016).

Jenkins, Henry. 2013. 'The Walking Dead: Adapting Comics,' in *How to Watch Television*, edited by Ethan Thompson and Jason Mittell, pp. 422–445. New York. New York University Press.

King, Stephen. 2004. *The Dark Tower Volume Six: Song of Susannah*. London: Hodder and Stoughton.

MacIntyre, Alasdair. 1985. *After Virtue: A Study in Moral Theory*. London: Duckworth.

Mittell, Jason. 2014. 'Strategies of Storytelling on Transmedia Television,' in *Storyworlds Across Media: Toward a Cross-conscious Narratology*, edited by Marie-Laure Ryan and Ian Noel-Thon, pp. 253–277. Lincoln, NE: University of Nebraska Press.

Mullane, Alex. 2018. 'Five Lessons that The Walking Dead Needs to Learn from Fear the Walking Dead's Big Reboot,' *Digital Spy* (May 9). www.digitalspy.com/tv/fear-the-walking-dead/feature/a856671/fear-the-walking-dead-season-4-time-jump-deaths/ (accessed July 14, 2018).

Proctor, William. 2013. 'Holy Crap!, More Star Wars! More Star Wars? What if They're Crap?: Disney, Lucasfilm and Star Wars Online Fandom in the 21st Century,' *Participations: Journal of Audience and Reception Studies* 10(1): 198–244.

Pustz, Matthew. 1999. *Comic Book Culture: Fanboys and True Believers*. Jackson, MI: University Press of Mississippi.

Reynolds, Richard. 1992. *Superheroes: A Modern Mythology*. Jackson, MI: University Press of Mississippi.

Ricoeur, Paul. 1984. *Time and Narrative*. Chicago, IL: Chicago University Press.

Ryan, Marie-Laure. 2014. 'Story/Worlds/Media: Tuning the Instruments of a Media-Conscious Narratology,' in *Storyworlds Across Media: Toward a Media-Conscious Narratology*, edited by Marie-Laure Ryan and Jan-Noël Thon, pp. 25–49. Lincoln, NE: University of Nebraska Press.

Ryan, Marie-Laure. 2018. 'Ontological Rules,' in *The Routledge Companion to Imaginary Worlds*, edited by Mark J.P. Wolf, pp. 74–81. London: Routledge.

Scolari, Carlos A. 2009. 'Transmedia Storytelling: Implicit Consumers, Narrative Worlds, and Branding in Contemporary Media Production,' *International Journal of Communication* 3: 586–606.

Tassi, Paul. 2015. 'There's Only One Character on The Walking Dead the Creator Says He Wouldn't Kill,' *Forbes* (October 18). www.forbes.com/sites/insertcoin/2015/10/18/theres-only-one-character-on-the-walking-dead-the-creator-says-he-wouldnt-kill/#167ca6f071ea (accessed July 12, 2018).

Wolf, Mark J.P. 2012. *Building Imaginary Worlds: The Theory and History of Subcreation*. London: Routledge.

2 Augmented Television
Sociological World-building

At the start of this book I implied that *The Walking Dead* was not merely a story about the nature of world-building, but equally one about world-fragmentation – narrativizing the regression of modern social life towards something more primitive. When we first enter this world, social distinctions are, allegedly, gone. In only the second episode of the television series, Rick Grimes lays out his revised worldview: 'Things are different now. . . . There's us and the dead. We survive this by pulling together, not apart.' While Rick's binary 'us-versus-them' mantra would become much more complex as time goes on, his notion of pulling together is relevant to the aims of this chapter, which considers how digital technology is used to enhance communication between a range of parties – producers and audiences, characters and actors – in ways that directly leads to world-creation value.

This chapter will explore the world-building practices that have been employed in augmenting the televisual experience of *The Walking Dead*. It looks at Internet content – namely *The Walking Dead: Red Machete*, a six-part webisode series available on AMC's website – as well as AMC's *Talking Dead* – a 30-minute accompanying talk show – and the AMC Story Sync facility, a double-screen application designed to enable audiences to post live comments about the episodes, respond to surveys, and talk to other audiences via a chat platform. In many respects, these three platforms best exemplify AMC's earlier mentioned channel brand strategy as that which works to 'give audiences something deeper, something richer, *something more*' (Goldberg, 2013). I will demonstrate how these three examples of what I call 'augmented television' draw on sociological and anthropological notions of communication, modern social life, and environment in ways that present opportunities for *sociological world-building*. Building on the previous chapter which examined world-building dynamics on a textual, discursive, and audience-based level, this chapter explores how world-building is shaped by uses and affordances of digital platforms and begins to push our discussions further towards audiences. Specifically, by drawing much more heavily on concepts from other fields – in this case, sociology and anthropology – I consider how these three media artifacts build the world of *The Walking Dead* by populating it with what Ryan calls *mental events*, i.e. how individual characters react to both actual and perceived events:

> Physical events cannot be properly understood without linking them to mental events. In the case of actions, these mental events are the motivations of the agents, and in the case of both actions and accidental events, such as earthquakes, they are the emotional reactions of the affected characters. Now if mental events are as much a part of a story as physical ones, then storyworlds are actually narrative universes made of . . . the beliefs, wishes, fears, goals, plans, and obligations of the characters.
>
> (Ryan, 2014: 36–37)

In this instance, it is useful to extend our discussion of the term 'characters' beyond mere on-screen fictional depictions by also analyzing the extra-diegetic iterations of these characters (i.e. the actors who play these characters and what they say about them publically), as well as the ways that audiences themselves become characters in the world of the story via the use of augmented television technologies and platforms. For that reason, a sociological approach – and social theory – becomes a fitting means via which to make sense of the world-building described throughout this chapter. Much social theory is rooted in the critical assumption that social order is not a linear or vertical process, i.e. where all macro forces 'drip down' to dictate operations of micro actions below, but instead acknowledges that social order is a feedback/feed-forward process where agents and structures mutually enact social systems as reciprocal cycles (see Giddens, 1984). Conceiving of world-building in this way – as a kind of sociology – allows us to consider the function of different digital platforms in affording aspects of fictional world-building based on a similar feedback/feed-forward cycle between producers and audiences (Freeman, 2016: 69–70). As will be analyzed via the aforementioned webisode series, chat show, and Story Sync app, these three platforms each offer sociological experiences whose world-building principles are founded on their heightened communicative affordances that in turn produce transmedia experiences based on emotion – or, rather, on the emotive reflection that is triggered by juxtaposing two temporally staggered media platforms.

Conceptualizing Augmented Television

Shortly I will delve into precisely what I mean by this idea of emotion-building or indeed analyzing the specifics of *The Walking Dead*'s augmented television platforms and their attempts at what I describe as sociological world-building via the likes of webisodes, talk shows, and Story Sync apps. But I will begin this chapter by outlining some of the key theoretical pillars needed to conceptualize transmedia world-building as an augmented televisual form, pointing to ideas of connected viewing and transmedia distribution.

So, first of all, what do I mean by 'augmented television'? Scholarly discussions in the present often concern the multi-platform potentials of the digital media economy (Holt and Sanson, 2014; Evans, 2011; Doyle, 2015). Jennifer Holt and Kevin Sanson (2014: 1), for instance, discuss 'connected viewing,' which refers to 'a multi-platform entertainment experience, and relates to a larger trend across the media industries to integrate digital technology and socially networked communication with traditional screen media practices.' From this, 'second screen' practices have materialized, where portable media devices, such as a smartphone or tablet, are used alongside the television screen to access online material that relates to televisual content. Companion apps such as those for the U.K.'s *The X Factor* (ITV, 2004–) provide gaming opportunities or additional behind-the-scenes material (see Evans, 2015; Evans, 2018a). For Evans (2015: 124), indeed, second screen artifacts demonstrate how fundamental transmedia practices have come to be for the television industry and its audiences; in particular, how transmedia strategies facilitate a form of 'mediated glance,' referring here to television's innate tendency to be 'treated casually rather than concentratedly' (Ellis, 1982: 128). This idea of users engaging with second screen artifacts via a 'mediated glance' will be explored in terms of its world-building value for the AMC Story Sync facility shortly.

But whereas important technological shifts towards connected viewing may have led in some cases to 'the migration of our media and our attention from one screen to many' (Holt and Sanson, 2014: 1), augmented television describes more than companion apps. We can think of 'augmented television' as an umbrella label, with 'connected viewing' merely one aspect of this larger practice. Beyond connected viewing, for instance, there is the much more traditional spin-off talk show, such as *The Xtra Factor* (2004–2015), a companion show to the aforementioned *The X Factor* broadcast on ITV2 in the U.K. straight after the main ITV show ends. Companion talk shows, broadcast as they are straight after episodes of their parent series, open up ideas of temporality in terms of our understanding of augmented television. Television, especially television broadcasting, is a fundamentally temporal medium. Even as changes such as streaming allow audiences to access television content whenever they choose, the temporal qualities of television persist. Television's liveness, its ability to broadcast events as they happen, is often held up as a defining characteristic of television broadcasting (Gripsrud, 1998; Carroll, 2003). Moreover, it is Raymond Williams' model of television as 'flow' that most usefully brings the temporalities of television together with the temporality of transmediality. 'Flow' has become one of the foundational models of television studies and is regarded as a defining characteristic of the medium itself (Gripsrud, 1998). The organization of television's flow into a schedule functions as a way to structure its endlessness (Ellis, 2000) and to frame program content for audiences (Weissman, 2017). According to Williams, the flow of related, unrelated, and semi-related content units is a planned part of television's structure (2003 [1974]: 93). Television, in essence, becomes a collection of different segments of content that are brought together into a larger whole and guided by an ever-present, though invisible, time-based organizational structure, as will be considered in terms of its world-building value for both *Red Machete* and *Talking Dead*.

Beyond the 'flow' of talk shows, webisodes are a perfect example of what Will Brooker (2004: 323) once described as 'television overflow'; that is, 'the tendency for media producers to construct a lifestyle experience around a core text, using the Internet to extend audience engagement.' For our purposes, it is useful to consider the form of the webisode in terms of digital distribution, i.e. to analyze when such content is made available online so to make sense of its world-building value. Alisa Perren argues that the changes wrought by digital technologies have placed a spotlight on the key area of concern when thinking about distribution: 'the ways that content moves through space (flows) and time (windowing)' (Perren, 2013: 167). In taking Perren's definition of digital distribution, the connections to transmediality become clear. Elizabeth Evans argues that transmedia logics are also about the ways in which content moves through space and time, explaining how 'the various ways in which transmediality manifests . . . are fundamentally tied to practices of distribution. Transmedia storytelling or marketing, for instance, rely on distribution strategies that carefully spread content across different media platforms and spaces' (2018b: 243).

Some of the distribution strategies of the media forms discussed in this chapter may be online, others may be broadcast more traditionally, but importantly they are all grounded in the workings of television. That is to say that they all often make use of innately live, ephemeral, and/or interactive digital affordances that open up transmedial environments based on practices of communication around and reaction to a television series. In effect, and as will now be explored, these forms of augmented television are all characterized by the crafting of a temporality based on reaction and reflection. So, let's first consider how this temporality works in terms of world-building dynamics in *The Walking Dead: Red Machete*.

The Walking Dead: Red Machete

Put most simply, cultural anthropology is the comparative study of the manifold ways in which people *make sense* of the world around them, while social anthropology is the study of the *relationships* among individuals and groups. As we shall see, *The Walking Dead: Red Machete* webisodes delve into character relationships, while the *Talking Dead* chat show helps audiences to make sense of the imaginary world in emotional terms. The AMC Story Sync app, meanwhile, does both. Anthropology is a broad, cross-cultural, and integrative discipline concerned with the environments in which people live and the material, social, and ideational cultures that serves as a buffer between human beings and the environment. Out of that broad framework comes a number of key anthropological concepts, such as 'adaptation,' which in this context focuses on understanding human societies in terms of how they react to and utilize the environments in which they live. Applying this anthropological concept of 'adaptation' to an analysis of world-building in *The Walking Dead: Red Machete* webseries becomes useful, since it extends ways of thinking about transmedia storytelling toward more sociological questions to do with how characters react to their fictional environments and, in particular, how the affordances of the webisode format open up opportunities for audiences to understand character relationships specifically via the 'flow' of their online release schedule.

The Walking Dead: Red Machete is a six-part story about the origins of the infamous red machete used by Rick to kill Gareth (Andrew J. West) during Season 5. Released during Season 8 of *The Walking Dead*, the webisode series, as AMC billed it, 'follows the path of a red-handled machete from its innocent beginnings on a hardware store shelf at the start of the apocalypse, as it lands in the hands of survivors good and evil, familiar and new.' Each of the webisodes, running approximately 3 minutes, were distributed on the AMC website roughly around a month or so apart between October 2017 and April 2018, coinciding the release of each new webisode with the broadcast date of particular episodes from Season 8.

The potential to release webisodes in almost any way, at any time, raises interesting questions to do with their narrative capabilities and, in our case, their world-building value. As transmedia producer Robert Pratten (2011) discusses, 'why do some web producers release their webisodes weekly? Why not release them two weeks apart or wait until enough episodes have been produced to release all at once or daily? Why not four hours apart or on demand?' Pratten's point is that the freedom of the webisode format means that there can be – and indeed should be – a clear creative reasoning behind the choice to schedule webisodes at particular times, a reasoning that goes beyond simply replicating the traditionally weekly broadcast schedule of television. At the same time, however, the practices of augmenting televisual content means structuring a relationship between different media platforms. As Evans puts it, 'the temporality of transmedia content (whether deliberately strategized or emerging more organically) is key to creating transmedia experiences. Transmediality is inherently *about* distribution' (2018b: 243). So what can the distribution choices of *The Walking Dead: Red Machete* tell us about world-building, particularly of mental events?

In short, and despite centering on an inanimate protagonist, i.e. a machete, as it moves from owner to owner, *The Walking Dead: Red Machete* is really a story about how characters emotionally react to loss and trauma, with its scheduling format encouraging viewers to reflect on the passing of time. Narratively, the webisodes embody the Giddensian concept of 'adaptation,' painting the world of *The Walking Dead* as a place where humans utilize the objects of their environment, e.g. a machete, in order to survive, but also in order to mourn, to remember, and to grow. For instance, in the opening chapter, 'Behind Us,' a character named Mandy (Anais Lilit) witnesses her younger sister devoured by a zombie; then, in the second chapter, 'Sorrowful,' her father is bitten by a zombie and dies off-screen. The story of these chapters, told mostly without dialogue, is thus one of mental events, centering on Mandy's emotional journey from shock, to trauma, to acceptance. Importantly, by staggering the release of these chapters over months, the viewer is denied the chance to witness this emotional journey in continuous terms; instead, a passing of time is imposed upon the viewer, at least for those who watched the webisodes when released. Moments from earlier chapters, such as Mandy's name being carving into the handle of the machete, are revisited in subsequent chapters, creating a space where past narrative events are reflected upon and remembered long after the fact, rather than just reacted to immediately, in ways that afford a stark emotional transformation for both the character and the audience based on time passing.

When examined through the lens of 'flow,' too, *The Walking Dead: Red Machete* webisodes can certainly be understood as working to frame the viewing experience of the main television episode content, but not necessarily narratively. The webisodes certainly fit the description of transmedia storytelling, where 'integral elements of a fiction [in this case, the origin story the red machete] get dispersed systematically across multiple delivery channels for the purpose of creating a unified and coordinated entertainment experience' (Jenkins, 2007). But the narrative of the red machete does not tie into the plot of Season 8, and nor is it intended to, despite the webisodes being released to coincide with the broadcast of a number of that season's episodes. We must therefore understand the relationship between Season 8 episodes and *The Walking Dead: Red Machete* less in terms of plot and more in terms of the televisual 'flow' of 'related, unrelated, and semi-related content units' (Williams, 2003 [1974]: 93). As noted above, all of these webisodes are mostly without dialogue, creating a visual style that, as their director Avi Youabian describes, is 'very musical, [making] the sound design score the actual narrative – and through editing, it builds to a crescendo and finally releases' (Grobar, 2018). The musicality of the webisodes encourages an emotional, rather than a cerebral, reaction, thus framing the experience of watching *The Walking Dead* across multiple media in emotional terms based on the organization of time. In effect, the distribution pattern of the webisodes allows audiences to make some kind of sense of the world of *The Walking Dead* in quite cultural anthropological terms. For example, one fan, documenting their thoughts on the webseries online, states: 'It makes you really think about how many other things that we don't even think about that the group has have been in other hands' (Walking Dead Forums, n.d.). Another fan notes: 'It really got me thinking about how the lives of characters are shaped by the journeys of everyone, or everything, around them' (Walking Dead Forums, n.d.). By focusing and returning to the object of the seemingly arbitrary red machete at different points in time, highlighting the change in the mental events of the characters around it, *The Walking Dead: Red Machete* webseries can be said to define a sociology for the storyworld: this world may be without civilized structure and order, but the actions of its characters and their emotional reactions still form meaning out of the chaos.

AMC Story Sync

This relationship between time, emotional reaction, and digital platform is augmented even further via AMC's online Story Sync application. The AMC Story Sync is used during the premiere of new episodes of *The Walking Dead*, beginning life in 2012. It promises audiences the opportunity to 'interact with the show while watching the premiere broadcast of the latest episode of AMC's *The Walking Dead*. Join the community of fans in weighing characters' decisions, rating the gore and rewatching intense scenes.' The Story Sync includes trivia questions, polls, exclusive videos, and pictures that relate to the new episode being broadcast, affording immediate reaction and interaction. Given the fact that the fictional milieu of *The Walking Dead* is so devoid of the sorts of media communication technologies characterizing this particular chapter's object of study, there is an ironic tension in place between the ways in which characters have become accustomed to reacting to fictional events on screen and the ways via which audiences can now communicate with others about those fictional events. This tension is why it is so useful to turn to sociology or anthropology when making sense of *The Walking Dead*'s world-building, for, broadly, these disciplines seek to grasp the full range of human experience, including the ways in which people react to circumstances.

In essence, the AMC Story Sync app affords world-building via what Anthony Giddens famously theorized as 'reflexivity' in sociological terms. For Giddens (1991: 16), there are three main elements that explain 'the peculiarly dynamic character of modern social life,' with 'reflexivity' being one of these. According to Giddens (1991), with the advent of new technologies the modern individual can no longer rely on prescribed social truths or predetermined life trajectories but has to reflect upon information, recommendations, norms, and ideals emanating from a variety of (mediated) sources. In other words, Giddens' notion of reflexivity is really speaking to much the same social processes that become tied to Ellis' aforementioned idea of the 'mediated glance' in televisual terms, since the 'modern individual,' aka the television viewer, is now able to look across a variety of screens and digital interfaces when engaging with, say, an episode of *The Waking Dead*, and must, in turn, be prepared to reflect on what they see. Said episode may well be 'treated casually rather than concentratedly' (Ellis, 1982: 128) in the sense that viewers are glancing to and from the episode itself alongside a range of other second-screen practices, but the narrative information gained during a mediated glance to and from the AMC Story Sync app carries significant world-building value, working to reinforce or contextualize character choices.

Consider an example. Season 7's premiere episode, 'The Day Will Come When You Won't Be,' was a particularly intense experience for audiences, featuring as it did the death of both Glenn (Steven Yeun) and Abraham (Michael Cudlitz) at the hands of Negan. The episode also sees Rick emotionally tortured by Negan, required to play fetch with an axe amongst a hoard of zombies before coming close to being forced to cut off his own son's arm with said axe. Accompanying the broadcast of this episode, the AMC Story Sync app in one sense gives insight into the motivations of the characters. The app begins, for example, with a quote from Rick from Season 5: 'There's a compound bow and a machete with a red handle. That's what I'm gonna use to kill you.' The confident, threatening quote juxtaposes with the image of Rick seen during the Season 7 opener, where he appears emotionally broken by the deaths of his friends and submissive to Negan's demands. In effect, the quote presented via the Story Sync app is like a transmedial equivalent to having a flashback within the episode, denoting Rick's and Negan's motivations as essentially the same. Elsewhere, features on the Story Sync are very much emotion-orientated, asking viewers, for example, to vote whether they are more frightened to find out about what just happened or what is about to happen.

As with Giddens' notion of social reflexivity more broadly, some of the Story Sync's features may appear to be banal, such as still images taken from the episode, while others point to more life-encompassing decisions that give shape to the storyworld's mental events. Even the still 'freeze frame' images within the Story Sync app, such as one shot of Negan thrusting his axe into the face of a physically and emotionally battered Rick, hold significant world-creation status. Kevin Moloney (2018: 181) talks about the role of photography as 'one of many media forms a producer might use in a transmedia project.' It is perhaps less simple to understand a photograph as being something more than a mere illustration of a point made in another media form, but the photograph is a self-contained story; it works independently of its companion media forms as much as it complements them. Moloney, in fact, shows how a photograph – a single media image – is capable of bringing together both actual and imagined narrative moments and spaces that co-exist and extend, in the viewer's mind, at least, beyond the borders of the photograph itself. Moloney (2018: 181–182) argues that for producers of trans-media projects in any genre, 'the critical thinking about photographs must not only be how they interact with other media forms used in a project, but how they are also autonomous stories, capable of rich, immersive narrative, fine detail and visual fact presentation.'

In the case of the aforementioned freeze-frame image of Negan thrusting his axe into Rick's face, for example, the image deliberately forces the viewer to focus on something that otherwise might have been merely glanced at on television. Negan's goal and motivation to emotionally destroy Rick and abolish his sense of leadership are emblemized in this image, as is his belief in his own dominance over anyone who threatens him. The greatest storytelling strength of this image is its intensity, capturing Negan in close up in a way that denies the viewer a means to escape from the intensity of the television episode, and instead further engulfs the viewer in the drama, brutality, and violence depicted in the television episode by denying the chance to glance elsewhere. Such freeze frames are not merely accompanying images, or even entry points into the storyworld, but are transmedia stories in their own right.

In another case, for example, the Story Sync includes a 'flashback' feature, which in this instance revolves around a set of black-and-white still images of the characters, scattered across the screen and, crucially, depicting moments of laughter for characters such as Glenn and Abraham. Colin B. Harvey (2015) argues that memory is always important to transmedia storytelling, given that audiences are required to remember the specificities of characters and events when they migrate across multiple media. But in this case the images directly shape how viewers react emotionally to the deaths of Glenn and Abraham in the television episode, reminding audiences of moments of prior happiness that jar uncomfortably with the sight of their violent deaths. While the images dramatized on television prioritize emotions of shock, the still photographs available via the Story Sync encourage feelings of melancholy and loss. In other words, it is not so much a fictional narrative that is being constructed transmedially across television and the Story Sync app as it is the emotional reactions of the audience. As one fan, surveyed for the purposes of this book, asserted: 'The second screen experience of the Story Sync lets you immediately contemplate what is happening on screen, that second.' Encouraging such heightened emotional engagement is achieved by all sorts of strategies, such as designing features on the Story Sync that force users to empathize with a particular character. For example, accompanying the Season 6 episode 'No Way Out' the Story Sync asked users: 'Who are you most like?,' with images of the cast available to choose from.

As the Story Sync goes on, the user answers a range of questions based on their own mental events, i.e. their motivations, preferred actions, and emotional reactions. Only at the end of this particular Story Sync did the user discover which of the characters they resemble the most and, importantly, whether their personal motivations, actions, and emotional reactions would have seen them surviving the events of the episode or not. This kind of live, interactive feature cannot help but encourage users to reflect deeply on their own individual life choices, raising questions about how our inner ideals may fit into a predetermined life trajectory. Far beyond Harvey's more individualized idea of transmedia memory based on remembering aspects of plot during the process of migrating across media, the AMC Story Sync app represents a form of transmediality based on exploiting the juxtaposition of narrative past and narrative present, such is the 'reflexive and self-organizing potential of transmediality on the level of culture, [as] each additional version of a text or its fragment influences the ways in which we understand and remember the source text itself' (Ibrus and Ojamaa, 2018: 90).

Other features include viewers being able to vote on how they would have responded to actions or choices depicted during the episode. In the 'The Day Will Come When You Won't Be' episode, Negan tests Rick's determination to escape by leaving his axe in a reachable position. On the Story Sync app, viewers then voted whether or not they 'would have grabbed the axe, too . . . ,' with 54% believing this action was 'worth a shot' compared to 44% who would have waited had they been in the same position. This voting system sets up what can be described as a kind of collective intelligence for how to behave and react in the world of *The Walking Dead*. The voting tool may not provide any further insight into Rick's character beyond what can be gauged via the television episode, but it does create a sense of the mental events for what it would be like to actually live in this storyworld, with urges of survival (i.e. represented by the choice to reach for the axe) paired with 'kill shot' images on the Story Sync (in this case, of blood splattered across a windscreen) that establish this world as a place where inner motivations to survive are threatened as much by humans as zombies. Again, such an idea can be understood as part of the sociology of the storyworld, and it is one that is largely defined and communicated via the relationship between multiple media platforms. The 'collective intelligence' of the interactive Story Sync audience also works to clarify the inner beliefs, wishes, and goals of characters in cases where such motivations may be hidden or ambiguous, as they are in the case of Negan's torturous handling of Rick throughout the opening Season 7 episode. At one stage the Story Sync app asked viewers to cast their vote on whether 'Negan's mostly . . . ' 'seeing what Rick's got' (30%) or 'teaching him his place' (70%). In effect, reinforcing a particular reading of Negan's motivations via clear statistics based on the views of other, simultaneous audiences works to populate the storyworld with precise notions of what Ryan calls mental events, with audiences ultimately reinforcing particular motivations, emotional reactions, beliefs, wishes, and goals for the characters.

Talking Dead

With *The Walking Dead: Red Machete* webisodes augmenting the televisual experience of *The Walking Dead before* the live broadcast of each episode, and with the AMC Story Sync app augmenting this experience *during* the live broadcast of episodes, it is the role of *Talking Dead* – a live television chat show that discusses episodes of both *The Walking Dead* and *Fear the Walking Dead* with cast and crew members as well as celebrity guests – to continue augmenting this experience *after* the television episodes have come to an end. There is thus an integrative aspect to *The Walking Dead*'s augmented television platforms, one that aligns with the disciplinary ethos of sociology and anthropology, which both assume that *all* aspects of *all* people's experiences belong together as an indivisible subject of study. How, then, do the accumulated experiences of people – audiences, producers, on-screen, off-screen – work together to shape how individual characters react to both actual and perceived events?

The answer to this question lies in the way that *Talking Dead*, first broadcast in 2011 and now up to 150 episodes at the time of writing, effectively works to provide audiences with insights into the traumas and losses experienced by the characters in the television series. In that sense, and continuing with our Giddensian approach, *Talking Dead* affords world-building via what Giddens calls 'social disembedding,' itself another element to describe modern social life.

'Social disembedding' refers to the '"lifting out" of social relations from local contexts and their rearticulation across indefinite tracts of time-space' (Giddens, 1991: 18). This 'lifting out' of social relations is sustained by so-called 'expert systems,' which, according to Giddens, include professionalized forms of knowledge that stretches across boundaries and saturates the lifeworld in different parts of the world through technological innovations and provides advice given by various practitioners as experts (doctors, therapists, scientists, etc.), either directly or through media. Similarly, the structure of *Talking Dead* provides audiences with the opportunity to reflect upon information, recommendations, norms, and ideals emanating from a variety of (mediated) sources, namely the television series itself, but also the other discourses communicated across other channels. In effect, *Talking Dead* helps audiences to make sense of the storyworld in emotional terms.

Consider a 2014 episode that followed the broadcast of 'Coda,' the eight episode of the Season 5, airing on November 30. 'Coda' featured the death of Beth Greene (Emily Kinney) and the corresponding episode of *Talking Dead* featured actress Kinney herself, who discussed the real-life traumas that emerge from working on *The Walking Dead*, namely the sadness that comes from being killed off. As Kinney discussed during her interview:

> Shooting the episode was stressful, because you're not just leaving the character . . . I had a whole life out there, as we all do. . . . The thing is, it is a job, and I was dealing with all the things that you would deal with for any job that you're working on for a number of years, like I had an apartment out there. I had to deal with all those logistics of moving, getting rid of my apartment, plus knowing I won't see all my friends all the time. . . . So I had to deal with my real life while also wanting to give the kind of focus that I wanted to give to the show.

What is not apparent from the above transcript is the fact that Kinney was on the brink of tears during her interview, with host Chris Hardwick reassuring her throughout with tissues and comforting words: 'It's sad, it's okay.' There is thus a tenderness and humanism to *Talking Dead* that carries world-building value insofar as it contributes enormously to the emotional fallout and emotional reaction from the planned and accidental events depicted in either *The Walking Dead* or *Fear the Walking Dead*. It is, in effect, a space for cast, crew, and fans to reflect on and mourn the horrors that come *from* these two television series. The key to this idea lies in what host Hardwick says at the very end of his interview with Kinney: 'I think it's helpful for people to see you like this.' In other words, and as with the world-building of the AMC Story Sync app, *Talking Dead* also focuses on feelings of melancholy and loss, lifting out the emotional reactions of affected characters from the local context of a television episode and rearticulating these reactions, i.e. the world's mental events, across the indefinite tracts of a companion chat show. Once again, it is not so much a fictional narrative that is being constructed across platforms as it is the emotional reactions of those involved.

We can understand the 'flow' between *The Walking Dead* or *Fear the Walking Dead* to *Talking Dead* in similarly emotional terms, with AMC holding their audience's attention across these programs by providing opportunities for catharsis or closure that start in the former and end in the latter, using the chat show to contribute insights into the beliefs of the characters via the comments of the actors who portray them. For example, in another episode of *Talking Dead*, this one following the broadcast of 'Wrath,' the Season 8 finale where the 'all-out war' between Rick and Negan reaches its climax, actor Andrew Lincoln explains Rick's thought process during the fight scene where he decides to spare Negan's life:

> Well, it's the moment when [Rick] realizes that killing isn't gonna take the pain away . . . it's when he learns his lesson. It's really just vengeance up until that point and I think he realizes, when faced with killing Negan, where he's about to go, what he's about to become. And I think in that moment, that fleeting moment, that's when he decides that if he doesn't try to save [Negan's] life, it's over. So I think ultimately it is a story about restraint rather than revenge and love rather than hate, which has always been so integral to our show.

In that sense, *Talking Dead* clarifies Rick's inner but long-since-forgotten belief in the importance of rebuilding the civilization that once defined the world, augmenting the 'why' of a key mental event by contributing what Giddens might describe as a professionalized form of knowledge, i.e. with Lincoln operating here as the 'expert system' in a chain of transmedia content. And, upon hearing Lincoln's 'expert' views on the inner beliefs of Rick, audiences posted their reactions to these views on Twitter, which were then read out live on *Talking Dead* by Hardwick: 'Thank you, Andrew, I felt let down in the moment but I see now that you're right – Negan does need to live.' Clearly, audiences were able to learn and to make greater sense of particular mental events via the process of reflection that is itself afforded via the temporality of two pieces of television, with their liveness structuring this relationship. As another fan surveyed during research for this book reinforced: 'I am always watching the TV show with my phone in my hands, and I really like to search the Twitter hashtags to see how others feel.' The concept of 'flow' may have been threatened by new technologies, but *Talking Dead* entices people to experience the world of *The Walking Dead* live by constructing an 'in-the-moment' emotional temporality across multiple programs.

Conclusion

The contemporary television landscape is becoming increasingly characterized by streaming and other online strategies that allow access to television content via laptops, tablets, and smartphones. In some ways, the technologies via which we now engage with television content disentangle the watching of television from any particular temporality. Yet the likes of Netflix and Amazon operate as part of a television industry that equally adopts inherently transmedial approaches to distribution that work to augment these televisual experiences across platforms. And to paraphrase Evans (2018b) from earlier in the chapter, transmediality is about the strategically organized temporal relationships amongst a range of platforms and channels. This chapter has reiterated the importance of the relationship between a linear and clearly established viewing temporality (or televisual 'flow') and the affordances of what I have called augmented television platforms in understanding the value of these platforms in world-building terms. On the one hand, the innately live, ephemeral, and highly interactive digital affordances of the webseries, app, and chat show analyzed throughout this chapter work to build the storyworld – in this case, its mental events – via their communicative capabilities. As has been hinted at already, the depiction and fallout of mental events are highly suited to the nature of transmediality, since the former deals with cause-and-effect relationships between actions and their emotional affects, while the latter provides a structure for these actions/affects via an organized, temporal relationship between multiple platforms. As evidenced, this temporal relationship orchestrates the emotional reactions of audiences.

On the other hand, speaking more broadly, television is not just available at home through the television set; it has since expanded onto buses and trains, into cafés and waiting rooms. In other words, television has opened itself out to being shaped by and integrated with the daily practices of social (and sociological) conceptions. It is therefore logical to open up analyses of contemporary television and its world-building formations to the disciplines of sociology and anthropology, which explicitly serve to make sense of relationships between multiple groups of people and their ever-changing (communicative) environments. I have shown how the sociological concepts of 'reflexivity,' 'adaptation,' and 'social disembedding' become useful analytic tools for describing a particular sociological kind of world-building. These concepts should encourage one to rethink the building of imaginary worlds as a process based on memory and reflection, characterized profoundly by the passing of time.

References

Brooker, Will. 2004. 'Living on Dawson's Creek: Teen Viewer's, Cultural Convergence and Television Overflow,' in *The Television Studies Reader*, edited by Robert C. Allen and Annette Hill, pp. 569–580. London: Routledge.

Carroll, Noel. 2003. *Engaging the Moving Image*. New Haven, CT: Yale University Press.

Doyle, Gillian. 2015. 'Multi-platform Media and the Miracle of the Loaves and Fishes,' *Journal of Media Business Studies* 12(1): 49–65.

Ellis, John. 1982. *Visible Fictions: Cinema, Television, Video*. London: Routledge.

Ellis, John. 2000. *Seeing Things: Television in the Age of Uncertainty*. London: I. B. Tauris.

Evans, Elizabeth. 2011. *Transmedia Television: Audiences, New Media and Daily Life*. London: Routledge.

Evans, Elizabeth. 2015. 'Layering Engagement: The Temporal Dynamics of Transmedia Television,' *Storyworlds: A Journal of Narrative Studies* 7(2): 111–128.

Evans, Elizabeth. 2018a. 'Transmedia Television: Flow, Glance, and the BBC,' in *The Routledge Companion to Transmedia Studies*, edited by Matthew Freeman and Renira Rampazzo Gambarato. pp. 35–43. London: Routledge.

Evans, Elizabeth. 2018b. 'Transmedia Distribution: From Vertical Integration to Digital Natives,' in *The Routledge Companion to Transmedia Studies*, edited by Matthew Freeman and Renira Rampazzo Gambarato, pp. 243–250. London: Routledge.

Freeman, Matthew. 2016. *Industrial Approaches to Media: A Methodological Gateway to Industry Studies*. Basingstoke: Palgrave Macmillan.

Giddens, Anthony. 1984. *The Constitution of Society: Outline of the Theory of Structuration*. Cambridge: Polity Press.

Giddens, Anthony. 1991. *Modernity and Self-identity: Self and Society in the Late Modern Age*. Cambridge: Polity Press.

Goldberg, Lesley. 2013. 'AMC Rebrands With New Logo, Tagline,' *The Hollywood Reporter* (April 13). www.hollywoodreporter.com/live-feed/amc-rebrands-new-logo-tagline-431997 (accessed August 14, 2018).

Gripsrud, Jostein. 1998. 'Television, Broadcasting and Flow: Key Metaphors in TV Theory,' in *The Television Studies Book*, edited by Christine Geraghty and David Lusted, pp. 17–32. London: Hodder Arnold.

Grobar, Matt. 2018. '"Red Machete" Producers Add to "The Walking Dead" Lore, Examining Inanimate Protagonist,' *Deadline* (June 15). https://deadline.com/2018/06/the-walking-dead-red-machete-nick-bernardone-avi-youabian-interview-news-1202361192/ (accessed July 19, 2018).

Harvey, Colin. 2015. *Fantastic Transmedia: Narrative, Play and Memory Across Science Fiction and Fantasy Storyworlds*. Basingstoke: Palgrave Macmillan.

Holt, Jennifer and Sanson, Kevin. 2014. *Connected Viewing: Selling, Streaming and Sharing Media in the Digital Age*. London: Routledge.

Ibrus, Indrek and Ojamaa, Maarja. 2018. 'Estonia: Transmedial Disruptions and Converging Conceptualizations in a Small Country,' in *Global Convergence Cultures: Transmedia Earth*, edited by Matthew Freeman and William Proctor, pp. 83–98. London: Routledge.

Jenkins, Henry. 2007. 'Transmedia Storytelling 101,' *Confessions of an Aca-Fan: The Official Weblog of Henry Jenkins* (March 22). http://henryjenkins.org/2007/03/transmedia_storytelling_101.html (accessed September 30, 2017).

Moloney, Kevin. 2018. 'Transmedia Photography: Implicit Narrative From a Discrete Moment,' in *The Routledge Companion to Transmedia Studies*, edited by Matthew Freeman and Renira Rampazzo Gambarato, pp. 173–182. London: Routledge.

Perren, Alisa. 2013. 'Rethinking Distribution for the Future of Media Industry Studies,' *Cinema Journal* 52(3): 165–171.

Pratten, Robert. 2011. 'How to Improve Engagement With Your Webisodes,' *Transmedia Storyteller* (January 7). www.tstoryteller.com/how-to-improve-engagement-with-your-webisodes (accessed July 15, 2018).

Ryan, Marie-Laure. 2014. 'Story/Worlds/Media: Tuning the Instruments of a Media-Conscious Narratology,' in *Storyworlds Across Media: Toward a Media-Conscious Narratology*, edited by Marie-Laure Ryan and Jan-Noël Thon, pp. 25–49. Lincoln, NE: University of Nebraska Press.

Walking Dead Forums. n.d. www.walkingdeadforums.com/forum/ (accessed July 10, 2018).

Weissman, Elke. 2017. 'Watching CSI: A Study of British Audiences Watching Channel 5 and 5 USA,' *Critical Studies in Television: The International Journal of Television Studies* 12(2): 174–190.

Williams, Raymond. 2003 [1974]. *Television: Technology and Cultural Form*. London: Routledge.

3 Social Media

Religious World-building

Around the midway mark in *The Walking Dead*'s sixth season on television, the undead walkers have swarmed the Alexandria Safe-Zone. Enid (Katelyn Nacon), hiding in a nearby church, looks up and sees the words 'Faith without works is dead,' a proverb taken from a Bible passage in James 2:26. The proverb speaks of the belief that faith is demonstrated by the action we take, that a lack of works is synonymous with an unchanged or meaningless life. In effect, the proverb reinforces the idea that actions and beliefs are intertwined, and so, by extension, it seems reasonable to suggest that the actions of building imaginary worlds can be tied to the beliefs and faiths of its fictional characters and indeed those of its audiences.

This chapter will explore the world-building practices that have been employed in and across *The Walking Dead*'s social media platforms. Of particular interest to many media scholars in ways that builds directly on the previous chapter has been the role of social media in 'connecting' audiences to live television, 'amplifying' their collective voice, and harnessing their input in creative ways (Harrington et al., 2013). In this chapter, however, I seek to move beyond a view of social media as a mere complement to the primacy of television, and examine how the affordances of social media platforms can produce distinct world-building experiences and provide specific narrative contributions. I argue that social media channels present unique opportunities for what I call *religious world-building*. To clarify, I am not referring to any specific uses of the word 'religion,' i.e. that which loosely describes a belief in gods or a supreme being. Rather, I am referring to the way in which the affordances and uses of social media creates a set of ideas about, say, family, community, or right and wrong, which act as a kind of belief system for fans of the imaginary world. Thus while Chapter 2 began to push discussions towards the role of audiences on world-building dynamics, this chapter's focus on social media means that, as Paul Boothe (2018: 61) described it, 'uniting two disparate areas of scholarship – the techno-social development of digital media and the sociocultural development of fan studies' – is needed. As Boothe (2018: 57) elaborates, 'in this sense, what matters is not just what the [media platform] *does for/to its users*, but also what the *users do for/to the [platform]*.' Ike Picone (2017: 6) goes on to note that 'grounding argumentation in the tradition of audience studies and opening up recent advances in the field of (cross-)media research' allows researchers to renew and refresh their description of 'the practices in which people engage through media.' Studying audiences through the lens of imaginary world studies reveals the transformative properties of audiences as key members of a world-building dynamic, allowing us to engage in analyses of what Hasebrink and Hepp (2017) characterize as both the 'individual' and the collective 'social domain,' as will be explained in more detail throughout this chapter.

Specifically, by drawing on ideas from the field of religious studies, this chapter considers how three social media platforms – Facebook, Twitter, and Instagram – each build the world of *The Walking Dead* by populating it with what Ryan called *social rules and values*, i.e. the principles that determine the obligations of the characters, which are 'powerful sources of narrativity because [they] are opportunities for transgression and, consequently, a source of conflict' (Ryan, 2014: 35–36). As Ryan further explains of this particular concept:

> The individual aspirations of characters, for instance, may be incompatible with the laws of the group they belong to, or characters may belong to different competing values, and they may be forced to make a choice between these values. If we define *plot* as a transgression of boundaries, then a plot is made possible by the rules that define boundaries.
>
> (Ryan, 2014: 36)

In effect, then, the nature of Ryan's approach to social rules and values in storyworlds is in itself religious, based on complex belief systems: 'a common faith in something that gives meaning and purpose' (Fitzgerald, 2000: 3). And in other ways, too, the pervasive integration of social media into our everyday personal lives has led to scholars delineating the social media phenomenon as a new kind of 'digital religion' or 'online church' (Hutchings, 2016); its ritualistic daily practices amongst many users are akin to how 'anthropologists in fact use "religion" as virtually coterminous with "ritual"' (Fitzgerald, 2000: 4). With that in mind, I will argue in this chapter that the use of social media platforms in the context of the world of *The Walking Dead* works to both engage with and extend rules of *community*, which for fans become, in itself, a kind of faith. For as I have argued elsewhere, 'transmedia can enable not just the spreading of messages across multiple media, but equally the creation of a social fence around those messages, inviting participation and building a stronger community' (Freeman, 2016: 4). The world of *The Walking Dead* is all about building community, both narratively and – via the likes of its social media – in terms of its audience dynamics.

Conceptualizing Social Media

Faith as world-building, then, will be the focus of this chapter. But as with other chapters, it is first important to lay out some of the fundamental theoretical work on social media before analyzing how these platforms afford examples of what I describe as religious world-building. Broadly, the technological affordances of social media that have democratized media by integrating tools and functions, allowing the average user to capture and edit their own photos and record their own videos, facilitate user-generated content. The rise of social media platforms, affording ways to 'communicate and share,' is the key way via which social media platforms have been theorized (Gauntlett, 2011). The continuous changes in the uses of social media have played a major part in the 'contemporary adoption, absorption, and retention of new technologies' (Cunningham and Potts, 2009: 137), but they have also been key to the increasingly intertwined link between technology and daily life. Social media is itself fundamental to the presentation of more 'personal' and thus more interactive media messages that is itself key to understanding transmediality in more real-world terms.

Indeed, elsewhere I have argued that the future of transmedia studies is to consider the increasing mediatization of everyday life and to understand our personal lives as transmedia experiences (Freeman and Gambarato, 2018). Throughout this chapter I will explore how the inner beliefs of *Walking Dead* characters become mediatized as part of the everyday lives of social media users, building these characters phenomologically as a blend of knowledge and make-believe. Such a blend is itself nothing if not part of the fabric of what social media *is*, or rather what it *does*. Social media is a platform that practices and embodies the ideology of Tim O'Reilly's Web 2.0, a concept based on the web encouraging participation among users and being a place that enables and promotes 'sharing, collaboration and content creation' (McStay, 2010: 37–38). What an audience can or cannot do is partly determined by the technological qualities that exist in their media, and social media thrives on the enabling of collaboration, providing rich ways of building imaginary worlds for and with audiences.

Collaboration has existed long before the arrival of digital media. Written and literary works published in print media, while assumed to be authored by one person, have often been the result of 'intense social interaction' and collaborative efforts by 'one or more writers and editors' (Kristeva, 1980, cited in Golumbia, 2014: 57). The digital era has nevertheless seen collaboration become much more far-reaching than before, as many websites, especially Internet spaces powered by Web 2.0 technologies, provide the tools for collaboration, which is why many digital artifacts on the Internet today are created by more than one author (see Golumbia, 2014). The term 'collaboration' has often been confused with user-generated content or 'sharing' one's photos and videos, but the latter does not require having more than one individual producing said content (Hyde et al., 2012). But there must also be a 'layer of coordination' which aggregates multiple users' contributions or content 'into a new social object' (Hyde et al., 2012: 53–54), for example having numerous tweets be accumulated under a single hashtag on Twitter or getting many users to upload their pictures into a group album on a photo-sharing website.

These tasks demonstrate a small degree of collaboration on social media platforms and those 'coordinating mechanisms' (Hyde et al., 2012: 54) help maintain a sense of coherence and relatedness among the many contributions. Interactivity has certainly eased collaborative efforts on social media in other ways, by enabling 'interactive commentary' and letting users 'respond to original productions' elaborately and instantly in a way that connotes 'their own implication in the production process' and this can even be demonstrated in the simplest form of 'comment functions' on blogs, media-sharing websites, and social media platforms (Golumbia, 2014: 58; see also Gauntlett, 2011). According to Hyde et al. (2012: 61–64), collaboration can also be measured, namely via the extent of 'knowledge transfer' that occurs among the participants, especially when they ask for and share knowledge on the topic. The workings of social media collaboration will be explored in terms of their world-creation value later on in this chapter, looking specifically at fan-owned *Walking Dead* Facebook groups, including an examination of the extent to which knowledge about the social values of the storyworld is essentially transferred between the users of said groups.

In this respect, we have to consider social media practices – and, by extension, their shaping of world-building practices – from at least two different perspectives. Hasebrink and Hepp (2017) refer to these dual perspectives as the 'repertoire' versus the 'social domains' perspective. According to Hasebrink and Hepp (2017: 363), 'typically cross-media research focuses either on the individual *or* on the social domain,' i.e. on the journey and behaviors of the individual audience member as they migrate across and between media, or on the larger, often corporate, strategies of those who design and create the transmedia platforms in the first place. For the researcher choosing to focus on the first perspective, the 'individual,' cross-media use is characterized as a particular 'media repertoire': 'From the perspective of the individual, media repertoires are composed of media-related communicative practices by means of which individuals relate themselves to the figurations in which they are involved' (Hasebrink and Hepp, 2017: 363; also see Hasebrink and Domeyer, 2012). Hasebrink and Hepp's second perspective involves 'social domains' (e.g. media organizations, communities, etc.) that can be understood as communicative figurations characterized by a particular 'media ensemble' (Hepp and

Hasebrink, 2014). 'From the perspective of figurations,' Hasebrink and Hepp explain (2017: 363), 'media ensembles are characterized by the media-related communicative practices of the actors involved in the particular social domain under analysis.' Due to the two-way communicative affordances of social media, both perspectives are necessary in order to understand such media in everyday life, as will be considered further shortly.

But two-way communication is not the only change shaping current social media pages. Beyond social media environments leading to audiences not just consuming but also turning into 'curators and aggregators' of content (Schackman, 2013: 115) – something that will itself be interrogated shortly in terms of implications for world-building – advertisers and television networks alike now place importance on the 'shareability' of their social media content. Attempts to overcome the barriers of attention economy now depend on utilizing the most important aspects and features of social and mobile platforms, with advertisers often presenting more 'personal' rather than 'corporate' messages (Rowles, 2014: 123). As such, 'social seeding' – an online marketing process wherein enticing quality content is showcased on highly visible social platforms – has fast become an essential practice (Baylis, 2011: 113). How, though, does social seeding work to build knowledge about the social values of a storyworld? This question will be explored via AMC's official Instagram pages for *The Walking Dead* and *Fear the Walking Dead*, which themselves are populated with all sorts of photographs, images, videos, and 'interactive media-rich ads' (Rappaport, 2007: 136).

Commercially speaking, in fact, to adapt to the new environment and compete for audiences' attention, many advertisers have invested their promotional efforts in various creative ways into social media advertising; as of 2015, 96% of businesses market their brands and products through social media networking sites (Phua et al., 2016: 412). Be that as it may, Carlos A. Scolari, Mar Guerrero-Pico, and María-José Establés (2018: 49) argue that social media is 'the entrance point for transmedia fandom, lending a more dynamic television experience based on conversations and, importantly, on those conversations being sustained over time' (see also Mittell, 2015; Cascajosa Virino, 2016). Migration to social media, such as Twitter, provides audiences with different opportunities to connect not only with other audiences but also with the producers and marketing teams of their favorite series who initiate these conversations to encourage engagement (Proulx and Shepatin, 2012). With fans embracing live-tweeting, for example, social media has become an integral part of media fandom – a companion platform, if you will, to the kinds of augmented television platforms of the previous chapter – with channels and networks promoting the use of Twitter hashtags 'to channel user interaction with televised content' (Association of Internet Researchers, 2014: 1). Let's, then, explore how collaboration, social seeding, and indeed live-tweeting each open up world-building to religious dimensions on Facebook, Instagram, and Twitter.

Facebook

Analyzing forms of religious world-building first means describing what I mean by religion. As hinted above, I am not concerned with substantive definitions of religion, i.e. referring to the presumed subject matter of a religion, or with any particular religion itself. Rather, this chapter is interested in functional definitions of religion, which 'seek to define it in terms of what it does for those who subscribe to it' (Chryssides and Geaves, 2007: 14). Functionalist definitions of religion are particularly favoured in the field of sociology, which is useful insofar as a sociological approach thus allows me to extend the sorts of ideas about the role of audiences in building imaginary worlds that I raised in Chapter 2. One prominent sociologist of religion, J. Milton Yinger (1970: 12), defines religion thusly:

> Religion, then, can be defined as a system of beliefs and practices by means of which a group of people struggles with these ultimate problems of human life. It expresses their refusal to capitulate to death, to give up in the face of frustration, or allow hostility to tear apart their human aspirations.

Note that Yinger does not simply talk about 'beliefs' but about 'a system of beliefs': religious beliefs are not assortments of unrelated points, but hang together in a coherent way. Second, and most importantly, Yinger insists that practices are relevant to defining religion:

what religious believers *do* is just as important as what they believe, if not more so. And such practices are said to 'offer strength for living and consolidation in sorrow' (Chryssides and Geaves, 2007: 20). As Yinger (1970: 12) points out, religions offer hope, giving 'sustenance to their followers and encourage them to work for a better world.' Applying these particular approaches of religious studies to an analysis of world-building in a range of *Walking Dead* Facebook pages becomes fruitful, since it enables us to make sense of how the affordances of social media open up opportunities for audiences to collaborate together in further defining and extending the moral code of the storyworld, binding together as an online community that, as per a religious community, 'offers guidance for life in the form of a moral code' (Chryssides and Geaves, 2007: 1–2). It is nothing if not relevant to note at this stage that one possible derivation of the word 'religion' is the Latin *religere*, meaning 'to bind together.' So religion, as Emile Durkheim famously recognized, can be seen as a social phenomenon.

Further, understanding any number of *Walking Dead* Facebook pages as a similarly social phenomenon, i.e. as 'a conversation and maintenance of faith' (Chryssides and Geaves, 2007: 49), leads me to describing the ways in which said pages are used to draw attention to those who produce the television series, and in turn what it means to be a fan of the television series. Take one post on AMC's *Walking Dead* Facebook page from 2013, for example. Just two episodes into Season 4, *The Walking Dead* surpassed 20 million Facebook fans (at the time of writing this figure is now closer to 35 million). To celebrate this Facebook milestone, AMC released an exclusive, tongue-in-cheek image that warned users: '20 Million Are Now Infected.' The image showed a guarded wire fence, behind which a swarm of zombies are attacking, with the words presented as a warning sign as if placed there by the producers. Much like the *Talking Dead* episodes of the previous chapter provided a space for cast, crew, and fans to reflect on and mourn the horrors that come from the television series, this same fluidity between fact and fiction plays out on social media too: posts like the aforementioned '20 Million Are Now Infected,' essentially thanking the fans for their support, works to blend the real world of television production with the narrative world of the television series.

In other words, the affordances of social media actively encourage an ontological way of seeing a storyworld. But how does such a way of seeing the world of *The Walking Dead* via social media contribute new aspects of world-building? The answer to this question lies in the specificity of the storyworld. Kyle William Bishop (2010: 14) observes that 'the generic protocols of the zombie story include the collapse of societal infrastructures and the fear of other surviving humans.' These conventions are certainly central to *The Walking Dead*, but they become interesting when played out against the social infrastructures of today's social media platforms, which by definition privilege not the fear of other people but rather the outright closeness and connectivity of and between people. We can understand this tension in terms of the role of *media* in this particular storyworld. It was noted in Chapter 1 how 'radio and television represent organized society's failure to come to terms with the unfolding disaster in Romero's classic zombie films' (Cameron, 2012: 66), though here it becomes the role of social media platforms to clarify the moral code of the world of *The Walking Dead*, i.e. its principles, values, and social rules, and to position (social) media as itself key to achieving these moral principles, values, and social rules of togetherness collaboratively.

Consider 'The Walking Dead Fandom Universe,' a fan-owned Facebook group with over 18,500 individual members at the time of writing. As per Yinger's definition of religion, i.e. as that which expresses a refusal to 'allow hostility to tear apart their human aspirations,' the rules of this Facebook group state that 'Members are allowed to have differences of opinion and debate about it as long as it's done in a civil manner . . . No slander, racial, orientation, political or religion discrimination will be tolerated.' Fans use 'The Walking Dead Fandom Universe,' as well as many other Facebook pages like it, partly as a means of offering each other strength following distressing or morally troubling narrative events, with the community of fellow users giving hope in ways that resemble a religious community. Or to put it another way, fans use these Facebook pages as an opportunity to define the social rules and values of the storyworld during moments of stark character transgression. For example, in response to seeing the latest episode from Season 8 – itself narrating the brutal 'all-out war' between Rick and Negan – one fan posted: 'I'm sorry but after this episode. . . does anyone else feel like Rick is kind of becoming the villain. . .?'

Said post, likely intended to initiate a debate, also can be read as a concerned fan looking for reassurance in much the same way as some people may seek religion so to gain emotional benefits, 'like healing, or coping with disappointment or bereavement' (Chryssides and Geaves, 2007: 1–2). What ensued from this particular post, however, was an exploration of the nature of villainy in the world of *The Walking Dead*. 'Honestly Rick has been the villain for years now,' one fan commented, before another fan reinforced: 'I always saw Rick as a villain. He is a poor leader, gets too overwhelmed emotionally and is too liberal with his approach.' However, other fans took the opportunity to reassure the original poster of Rick's innate goodness: 'No, he's overwhelmed with grief, that's all.' Another remarked, emphatically: 'He's made some serious mistakes, no doubt, but Rick is an innately good guy to his group. He'll rebound.'

Importantly, however, while the thread may have begun by polarizing 'yes' and 'no' opinions on the question of whether Rick was becoming a villain, eventually it transitioned into one of many examples of how social media users collaborate together to establish and then maintain a coherency about the moral values of characters, in turn developing a set of beliefs and principles about the world of *The Walking Dead*. As one fan commented: 'I see [Rick] as trying his best to protect his people while dealing with all manner of monsters, both living and dead.' Another fan concurred: 'It's all about survival and how far you will go to live and keep others alive.' Suddenly, almost all user comments in the thread had agreed on how to best describe the amoral nature of the storyworld: 'It's never been about good guys vs bad guys. It's about what you'll do to survive and keep you and your people alive. Anyone who thinks it's good vs evil is sadly mistaken. Rick's no better than Negan or anyone else.' In one sense, this collectively formed definition of the storyworld's amoral fabric and the characters within it can be seen as another instance of what I discussed in Chapter 2 to be the world-creation value of the 'collective intelligence,' i.e. the role of users, in this instance via the affordances of social media, to clarify a shared understanding of the storyworld's morality.

Indeed, the various users of 'The Walking Dead Fandom Universe' page were each asked to share their knowledge and beliefs on the topic, and altogether they soon aggregated multiple users' contributions into what Hyde et al. (2012: 61) described earlier as 'a new social object': in this case, a written belief system, i.e. set of social rules and values, about the nature of right and wrong in the world of *The Walking Dead*. And this creation of a written belief system exemplifies the power of the individual in transmedia processes, whose 'media repertoires are composed of media-related communicative practices by means of which individuals relate themselves to the figurations in which they are involved' (Hasebrink and Hepp, 2017: 363). Indeed, these kinds of Facebook threads even operate as a form of 'knowledge transfer' between different individual users, a form of online collaboration that can be measured, in a sense, firstly via the numbers of 'likes' that a particular opinion receives and secondly via individual comments that, to various extents, acknowledge a change of belief in the values of the storyworld: 'Wow, although I would love for Rick to live with his own free will rather than under a spell of amorality, come to think of it, you're right about there being no time for democracy and freedom.' Essentially, then, this kind of online behavior is nothing if not akin to that of a small religious community – turning to social media 'for guidance for life in the form of a moral code' (Chryssides and Geaves, 2007: 1–2), curating and collaborating on content so to define a system of beliefs about the storyworld.

Instagram

These online practices of curation, aggregation, and collaboration are indeed akin to a set of religious beliefs, informing the individual what actions are good and desirable in the world of *The Walking Dead*, and which are bad and are to be avoided. Sociologists are interested in how certain social organizations like religions use this kind of information to establish power structures to uphold what they believe to be right (see Corrywright and Morgan, 2006). If applying this approach to the interests of this chapter, it becomes possible to describe official AMC social media channels as that which reinforce a particular set of ideas about, in this case, family, community, or right and wrong, and which further promote a set of social rules and values for fans of the storyworld. I will therefore now switch my attention to Hasebrink and Hepp's second perspective on cross-media behavior: what they call 'social domains' (e.g. media organizations, communities, etc.). This second perspective, as outlined above, puts emphasis on 'the media-related communicative practices of the actors involved in the particular social domain under analysis' (Hasebrink and Hepp, 2017: 363). As I will show, AMC's official Instagram pages for *The Walking Dead* and *Fear the Walking Dead* – with 6.6 million followers and 891,000 followers respectively at the time of writing – are social domains that carry world-creation value insofar as they work to clarify and illuminate the reasons to commit to the characters of these two series despite them often enacting transgressive, morally gray, and outright faith-shaking acts within the narrative. Doing so essentially means making use of social media's ability to cross the diegetic with the extra-diegetic, giving social media users more reason to believe in the reality of the storyworld.

Earlier I suggested that the affordances of social media encourage an ontological way of seeing a storyworld. To elaborate on this idea, one might attempt to theorize the aesthetics and properties of a social media page by pointing to the way in which these pages encourage users to go 'into the scenes' (diegetically) and 'behind the scenes' (extra-diegetically). So what does it mean for a social media page to go 'into the scenes' of imaginary worlds? In short, an 'into the scenes' aesthetic on social media is based on 'mashup, [operating] as a site of remix' (Kidd, 2014: 117). Matt Hills (2018), for instance – looking at how The Justified Ancients of Mu Mu and their instantaneous 'meta' fandom parodied notions of participatory consumption through social media – argues that these social media influencers 'worked with the industrial apparatus of popular music to playfully remix and re-narrate it' (Hills, 2018: 30).

What, though, is the world-creation value of this kind of social media remix, notably for a world's social rules and values? As a start, consider one fairly typical post from *The Walking Dead* Instagram page, dated October 19, 2015. Here, an image of Rick is captioned with the words: 'This is an insane world.' Then, just 1 week later, clearly intended as a follow-on to the previous post, a second image of Rick was posted, this time with the words: 'If something's in front of you, you kill it.' These words are of course moments of separate dialogue lifted from different episodes, but remixed such as they are across two juxtaposed posts on Instagram, it works to reinforce the belief system surrounding the storyworld's moral code, clarifying and justifying Rick's inner principles, social rules, and personal values.

One might thus point to the various religious-like practices on display on Instagram, as *Walking Dead* fans 'accumulate rituals, myths, codes of morals, clothing, texts, holidays, mass celebrations . . . and other ritual gatherings' (Wagner, 2012). However, Instagram does much more than merely reinforce a kind of belief system for the storyworld's principles and social values via diegetic, 'into-the-scenes' remixes; it also embeds new knowledge about this belief system that goes 'behind the scenes' and which is largely specific to the platform.

To clarify, there is a sense, as Marie-Ève Carignan and Sara Marcil-Morin (2018: 133) note, that social media works not to create a new aspect of transmedia communication per sé, but rather to 'spread a message and complete it . . . by relaying images and statements across various platforms.' So, which of *The Walking Dead*'s social rules and values are relayed and completed via 'behind-the-scenes' aesthetics on Instagram? In answering this question, it is notable that approximately 50% of the posts on both the @amcthewalkingdead and @fearwalkingdeadamc pages are images or videos of cast and crew, typically taken on set and between takes. Many of these types of posts are selfies featuring two or three cast members, while others are group photographs of a larger number of cast and crew huddled together. This group aesthetic also extends to posts of the same cast and crew together at parties and back stage at award ceremonies and talk shows. Such images are posted alongside stills from the television series themselves, many of which are captioned with social values, such as 'This is for my family.' In this sense, Instagram is a behind-the-scenes paratext in a similar vein to *Talking Dead*, focusing on the real-life actors from the television series and their apparent comradery with each other in ways that extends the storyworld's social values to do with family, trust, and community beyond the diegetic and into the extra-diegetic.

With Instagram, then – specifically the official AMC Instagram pages created for *The Walking Dead* and *Fear the Walking Dead* – quite often it is not an either/or binary between 'into-the-scenes' (diegetic) and 'behind-the-scenes' (extra-diegetic) aesthetics, but rather a combination of the two. For example, to introduce users to the character of John Dorie (Garret Dillhunt) on *Fear the Walking Dead*, the corresponding Instagram page gave users two posts within a couple of days of each other. The first post introduces John as 'The Gunslinger' with the caption: 'He doesn't want to kill. So don't make him #FearTWD.' The second post was captioned: 'He's a good man. But that won't stop him from putting you away #FearTWD,' with the words 'I did not want to kill anybody today' plastered across the image of the post. In one respect, this kind of post exemplifies how transmedia audience behavior crosses from what Hasebrink and Hepp (2017) described as the 'individual' to the 'social domains,' with the kinds of social values to do with the storyworld's amoral fabric that were debated and agreed by individual Facebook users here becoming solidified by the social domain of AMC. But much more than this, what is immediately apparent about both of these introductory posts for the John Dorie character is their *look*. Which is to say that the footage of the character is not taken from the television series ('into-the-scenes'), nor is it a behind-the-scenes interview with the actor. Instead, it is clearly an in-character video of John Dorie, but one that emphasizes the artifice of the scenario: Dorie is shot, in long lens, against a white wall, with the flashes of the photographer's light clearly and deliberately captured. The effect is a kind of 'magic realism' for the age of social media, expressing a primarily fictionalized view of the storyworld while also adding and reveling in real-world elements.

From a marketing standpoint, this kind of 'magic realism aesthetic,' if you will, is nothing if not an example of social seeding, with the aforementioned Instagram posts embodying an engaging visual style that becomes a form of quality content for users. The impact of this visual style in world-building terms is that particular social rules and values, i.e. those that are especially significant to the quality of the brand, become presented in such a way that they are perceived as much more than mere fiction – they become more *real*, as it were, seemingly defining the beliefs of the actors as much as those of their characters.

Ascribing the world-creation value of social media as that which reinforces a 'real' belief system and articulates the inner principles, values, and social rules of characters is itself emblematic of the affordances of the medium, especially when paired with the medium of television. For example, Gerbner et al. (2002: 194) compares religion and television, noting:

> Television provides, perhaps for the first time since the preindustrial religion, a daily ritual that elites share with many other publics.

The heart of the analogy of television and religion, and the similarity of their social functions, lies in the continual repetition of patterns (myths, ideologies, 'facts,' relationships, etc.) that serve to define the world and legitimize the social order.

More than repeating the patterns of the storyworld's social order, Instagram – by drawing attention to the fictionality or innate artifice of the storyworld in the way I describe above – creates a scenario whereby audiences are in a position to engage with fictional social rules and values in much the same way as they engage with their own lives, with images that only further augment fantasy into reality. In other words, social media establishes a religious-like scenario where audiences are able to believe in the world of *The Walking Dead* even more.

Rather like a Christian pilgrimage, perhaps, visiting the @amcthewalkingdead and @fearwalkingdeadamc Instagram pages is itself a journey for audiences, a physical migration across media and a proverbial journey to a 'magic realism' extension of the storyworld, one that serves to reinforce and strengthen a sense of fandom. For journeying to these particular social media sites means engaging with images and messages that break out of fictionality and become spiritually significant insofar as they become something more real. They emerge as sites where cast and crew step outside of their fictional trappings and allow audiences to encounter their extra-diegetic selves, ascribing a sense of real-world weight to the social rules and values depicted across both ontological terrains. And in that sense, Instagram becomes an important transmedial extension of the storyworld: a place where beliefs are heightened.

Twitter

Looking across to another social media platform – in this case, Twitter – it becomes apparent that not only does social media have the power to heighten users' beliefs in a storyworld, it also has the potential to condone or even to challenge a storyworld's social rules and values. The @WalkingDead_AMC Twitter page is notable for its sheer popularity. At the time of writing, *The Walking Dead* has 6.9 million followers on Twitter. In an average 30 day period (especially when coinciding with the start of a new season), the @WalkingDead_AMC Twitter page posts over a thousand tweets, a figure that is far higher than the average for US television series (Gottke, 2015). The Season 4 premiere of *The Walking Dead* generated some 1.2 million tweets, attracting a Twitter audience of nearly 7.5 million (Kain, 2018). This vast scale and degree of engagement means that it is useful to combine Hasebrink and Hepp's 'individual' versus 'social domains' perspectives. The first section of this chapter focused primarily on the former perspective, i.e. on the behaviors of the individual audience member on Facebook, while the second section dealt more so with the latter, i.e. on AMC's corporate Instagram strategies. This final section will therefore interlace both perspectives to help, as Hasebrink and Hepp (2017: 363) put it, 'clarify the conceptual and empirical relationship between media use as individual [user] practice *and* as part of an [industrial] figuration.'

Indeed, if the first part of this chapter showed how individual Facebook posts can clarify the moral code of a storyworld, and the second part of the chapter argued that the aesthetics of an Instagram post can allow users to believe in the reality of a storyworld more profoundly, then in this final section I will demonstrate how a simple hashtag on Twitter can carry with it all sorts of complex moral principles to do with the tensions between characters, with the act of live-tweeting leading to certain moral principles being condoned over others.

Much like the practice of social seeding discussed previously, live-tweeting has become a dominant marketing strategy associated with increasing audience engagement. One such strategy in the world of *The Walking Dead* has been for the producers to post hashtags at the bottom of the screen that Twitter users can tweet while watching the latest episode. These hashtags create engagement and conversation not only between the series and its audiences but fellow audiences alike. It also leads to trending hashtags, such as a word or phrase, which encourages many Twitter users to post the hashtag in or as their own tweet. For example, on October 20, 2013, accompanying Season 4 episodes was the hashtag #TheWalkingDeadin5, which became a trending topic on Twitter in a matter of seconds, 5 minutes before the new episode was set to begin. In addition, other suggested hashtags were then presented on screen throughout the episode to encourage audiences to search that particular hashtag as well as to use it when posting their opinions and reactions to what was going on in the episode.

An example of one such content-related trending hashtag that brought with it unique world-creation value would be #InCarolWeTrust, which the @WalkingDead_AMC Twitter page announced as 'our new motto' on October 19, 2015. This followed an episode from Season 6 titled 'JSS,' where Carol killed a large number of invading Wolves – a group of deranged attackers – who had scaled the walls of the Alexandria Safe-Zone and began killing anyone they saw. The proud declaration of the #InCarolWeTrust motto meant that Carol's belief that the Wolves must be killed became, in effect, condoned by the social domain that is AMC. But condoning Carol's killing is nothing if not ironic given the character's history. Back in Season 4, with the flu outbreak getting worse at the prison, Rick and Carol hit the road in search of their own medical supplies. After finding supplies and food, Rick and Carol began to address her earlier decision to kill Karen (Melissa Ponzio) and David (Brandon Carroll). In the episode 'Indifference,' Carol maintains that she did what was necessary to prevent the spread of the virus, while Rick believes that Karen and David deserved the chance to recover. Ultimately, Rick makes the decision to effectively banish Carol from the group, telling her that she can no longer be trusted and demands that she travel alone.

Morally, Carol's reasoning to kill raises the same kinds of ethical questions that fans had raised about Rick, as demonstrated by the earlier 'is Rick becoming a villain?' thread on Facebook. In that instance, individual users made use of a Facebook fan group to essentially curate, aggregate, and collaborate to establish what I described as a kind of 'new social object' (Hyde et al., 2012: 61): a written belief system, i.e. a set of social rules and values, about the nature of right and wrong in the world of *The Walking Dead*. Importantly, all of the user comments in that Facebook thread which had collectively agreed on a description of the amoral nature of the storyworld (as a place not about 'good guys vs bad guys,' but one 'about what you'll do to survive and keep you and your people alive') suddenly are carried over and infused into #InCarolWeTrust. Thousands of individual users have since used this hashtag as a sign of support for the violence enacted by the character; if Yinger's (1970: 12) definition of religion hinges on the 'practices by means of which a group of people struggles with [the] ultimate problems of human life,' then, most fundamentally, #InCarolWeTrust affords world-building via its ability to imply a transformation in this 'new social object' being a fannish activity to being something more akin to a social domain. Ryan's conception of social rules and values refers precisely to the same kinds of moral tensions as the feud between Rick and Carol described above: 'characters may belong to different competing values, and they may be forced to make a choice between these values' (2014: 36). The use of Twitter hashtags, such as #InCarolWeTrust, thus ultimately extends these social rules and values by presenting a quasi-vindicated stance on the amorality of the storyworld, offering a kind of guidance for life in the form of a moral code, bringing people together as a loyal, hopeful, belief-filled community. For as Stine Lomborg and Mette Mortensen (2017: 7) write: 'Cross-media use is not only a question of the availability of communication sources. It also concerns the users' orchestration of the media menu to select, consume, share and take action on information.'

Conclusion

The consumption of media content from the world of *The Walking Dead* – much like that of Hollywood franchises such as *Star Wars, Harry Potter*, and *The Hunger Games* (see Wagner, 2012; Ringlestein, 2013) – can be compared to a form of religiosity closely linked with the transmedial consumption of ideological content relating to the inner beliefs of characters. As Rachel Wagner (2012: 208) explains, we should 'think of transmedia as religion, and religion as transmedia in the way that they both provide ways of negotiating with the mediums [*sic*] of life with the goal of unification and actualization of ultimate reality' (see also Ringlestein, 2013). Meanwhile, other scholars, such as Marie-Ève Carignan, have researched how recent 'industrial developments have allowed religions to assume a strategic transmedia approach in a way that allows them to make use of new and different media so to develop a more complex and complete message' (2018: 366). One key media development in this process is of course social media, whose affordances 'mean that more is possible' (Molloy, 2017).

This chapter has reiterated these kinds of conceptual overlaps between notions of religion and aesthetics and practices of social media platforms, showcasing the value of applying religious studies ideas to these platforms when investigating world-building. On the one hand, with users invited to go both 'into the scenes' and 'behind the scenes' of the world of *The Walking Dead*, social media presents a cross-ontological opportunity for the once-fictionalized moral views of characters to become real and made coherent via online discussion, debate, and curation; online users collaborate together to maintain that sense of coherency for the storyworld, in turn developing a working set of beliefs that carry forward across multiple posts and channels. On the other hand, I have demonstrated how different forms of social media can function to give moral guidance and hope following distressing narrative events or to condone particular moral perspectives, cementing a particular set of beliefs about characters who may well belong to different or competing social values, with the actions of fellow users given a key role to play, much like in a religious community.

It is therefore logical to open up analyses of world-building to the discipline of religious studies, but also to community media, whose ideas of 'tradition, access . . . and public participation' (Howley, 2005: 121) become equally applicable to the social media-specific world-building analyzed in this chapter. If community media refers most broadly to initiatives 'dedicated to the principles of free expression and participatory democracy, and committed to enhancing community relations and promoting community solidarity' (Howley, 2005: 2) then in this chapter I have pinpointed some of the ways in which the 'adoption, absorption, and retention of social media technologies' (Cunningham and Potts, 2009: 137) provide a space for a community of online users to help, to heal, and to guide. This religious approach should cause one to rethink the building of imaginary worlds as a process based on collaborative moral debate, characterized by the blending of diegetic and extra-diegetic aesthetics in ways that work to immerse a set of fictional belief systems into everyday life.

References

Association of Internet Researchers. 2014. 'Social TV: Quantifying the Intersections between Television and Social Media,' *Selected Papers of Internet Research 15: The 15th Annual Meeting of the Association of Internet Researchers*, pp. 1–23. Daegu, Korea: Association of Internet Researchers.

Baylis, Catherine. 2011. 'Is Peep Culture the New Pop Culture?,' in *Digital Advertising: Past, Present, and Future*, edited by Daniele Fiandaca and Patrick Burgoyne, pp. 109–114. UK: Creative Social.

Bishop, Kyle William. 2010. *American Zombie Gothic: The Rise and Fall (and Rise) of the Walking Dead in Popular Culture*. London: McFarland & Company.

Boothe, Paul. 2018. 'Audience and Fan Studies: Technological Communities and Their Influences on Narrative Ecosystems,' in *Reading Contemporary Serial Television Universes: A Narrative Ecosystem Framework*, edited by Paola Brembilla and Ilaria A. De Pascalis, pp. 57–73. London: Routledge.

Cameron, Allan. 2012. 'Zombie Media: Transmission, Reproduction, and the Digital Dead,' *Cinema Journal* 52(1) (Fall): 66–89.

Carignan, Marie-Ève. 2018. 'Transmedia Religion: From Representations to Propaganda Strategy,' in *The Routledge Companion to Transmedia Studies*, edited by Matthew Freeman and Renira Rampazzo Gambarato, pp. 364–372. London: Routledge.

Carignan, Marie-Ève and Marcil-Morin, Sara. 2018. 'Canada: Transmediality as News Media and Religious Radicalization,' in *Global Convergence Cultures: Transmedia Earth*, edited by Matthew Freeman and William Proctor, pp. 121–139. London: Routledge.

Cascajosa Virino, Concepción. 2016. *La Cultura de las Series*. Barcelona: Laertes.

Chryssides, George D. and Geaves, Ron. 2007. *The Study of Religion: An Introduction to Key Ideas and Methods*, 2nd edn. London: Bloomsbury.

Corrywright, Dominic and Morgan, Peggy. 2006. *Religious Studies*. Edinburgh: Edinburgh University Press.

Cunningham, Stuart and Potts, Jason. 2009. 'New Economics for the New Media,' in *Mobile Technologies: From Telecommunications to Media*, edited by Gerard Goggin and Larissa Hjorth, pp. 131–142. London: Routledge.

Fitzgerald, Timothy. 2000. *The Ideology of Religious Studies*. Oxford: Oxford University Press.

Freeman, Matthew. 2016. 'Small Change – Big Difference: Tracking the Transmediality of Red Nose Day,' *View: Journal of European Television History and Culture* 5(10): 87–96.

Freeman, Matthew and Gambarato, Renira Rampazzo. 2018. *The Routledge Companion to Transmedia Studies*. London: Routledge.

Gauntlett, David. 2011. *Making Is Connecting: The Social Meaning of Creativity, from DIY and Knitting to YouTube and Web 2.0*. Cambridge: Polity Press.

Gerbner, George, Gross, Larry, Morgan, Michael, and Signorielli, Nancy. 2002. 'Growing Up with Television, the Cultivation Perspective,' in *Against the Mainstream: The Selected Works of George Gerbner*, edited by Michael Morgan, pp. 193–213. New York: Perter Lang.

Golumbia, David. (2014) 'Characteristics of Digital Media,' in *The Johns Hopkins Guide to Digital Media*, edited by Marie-Laure Ryan, Lori Emerson, and Benjamin J. Robertson, pp. 54–59. Baltimore, MD: Johns Hopkins University Press.

Gottke, Julia. 2015. 'Homeland vs. The Walking Dead: A Social Media Battleground,' *Quintly* (October 30). www.quintly.com/blog/homeland-vs-the-walking-dead-social-media (accessed August 14, 2018).

Harrington, Stephen, Highfield, Tim, and Bruns, Axel. 2013. 'More than a Backchannel: Twitter and Television,' *Participations: Journal of Audience and Reception Studies* 10(1): 405–409.

Hasebrink, Uwe and Domeyer, Hanna. 2012. 'Media Repertoires as Patterns of Behaviour and as Meaningful Practices: A Multimethod Approach to Media Use in Converging Media Environments,' *Participations: Journal of Audience and Reception Studies* 9(2): 757–783.

Hasebrink, Uwe and Hepp, Andreas. 2017. 'How to Research Cross-media Practices? Investigating Media Repertoires and Media Ensembles,' *Convergence: The International Journal of Research into New Media Technologies* 23(4): 362–377.

Hepp, Andrea and Hasebrink, Uwe. 2014. 'Human Interaction and Communicative Figurations: The Transformation of Mediatized Cultures and Societies,' in *Mediatization of Communication*, edited by Knut Lundby, pp. 249–271. Berlin: de Gruyter.

Hills, Matt. 2018. 'United Kingdom: The Justified Ancients of Mu Mu's "Comeback" as a Transmedia Undertaking,' in *Global Convergence Cultures: Transmedia Earth*, edited by Matthew Freeman and William Proctor, pp. 19–37. London: Routledge.

Howley, Kevin. 2005. *Community Media: People, Places, and Communication Technologies*. Cambridge: Cambridge University Press.

Hutchings, Tim. 2016. *Creating Church Online: Ritual Community, and New Media*. London: Routledge.

Hyde, Adam, Linksvayer, Mike, Kanarinka, Peirano, Marta, Tarka, Sissu, Taylor, Astra, Toner, Alan, and Zer-Aviv, Mushon. 2012. 'What Is

Collaboration Anyway?,' in *The Social Media Reader*, edited by Michael Mandiberg, pp. 53–67. New York: New York University Press.

Kain, Erik. 2018. 'Fear The Walking Dead Season 4, Episode 1 Review: What's Your Story?,' *Forbes* (April 15). www.forbes.com/sites/ erikkain/2018/04/15/fear-the-walking-dead-season-4-episode-1-review-whats-your-story/#21e1495a71ea (accessed August 3, 2018).

Kidd, Jenny. 2014. *Museums in the New Mediascape: Transmedia, Participation, Ethics*. Farnham: Ashgate.

Lomborg, Stine and Mortensen, Mette. 2017 'Users across Media: An Introduction,' *Convergence: The International Journal of Research into New Media Technologies* 23(4): 343–351.

McStay, Andrew. 2010. *Digital Advertising*. Basingstoke: Palgrave Macmillan.

Mittell, Jason. 2015. *Complex Television: The Poetics of Contemporary Television Storytelling*. New York: New York University Press.

Molloy, M. 2017. 'Sherlock Live: Fans Challenged to Solve Live Twitter Mystery,' *The Telegraph* (January 11). www.telegraph.co.uk/ tv/2017/01/10/sherlock-live-fans-get-chance-solve-exciting-mystery-live/ (accessed February 16, 2018).

Picone, Ike. 2017. 'Conceptualizing Media Users across Media: The Case for "Media User/Use" as Analytical Concepts,' *Convergence: The International Journal of Research into New Media Technologies* 23(4): 378–390.

Phua, Joe, Jin, Seunga Venus, and Kim, Jihoon. 2016. 'Gratifications of Using Facebook, Twitter, Instagram, or Snapchat to Follow Brands: The Moderating Effect of Social Comparison, Trust, Tie Strength, and Network Homophily on Brand Identification, Brand Engagement, Brand Commitment, and Membership Intention,' *Telematics and Informatics* 34: 412–424.

Proulx, Mark and Shepatin, Stacey. 2012. *Social TV: How Marketers Can Reach and Engage Audiences by Connecting Television to the Web, Social Media and Mobile*. Hoboken, NJ: John Wiley.

Ringlestein, Yonah. 2013. 'Real or Not Real: The Hunger Games as Transmediated Religion,' *Journal of Religion and Popular Culture* 25(3): 372–387.

Rowles, Daniel. 2014. *Mobile Marketing: How Mobile Technology Is Revolutionizing Marketing, Communications and Advertising*. London: Kogan Page.

Ryan, Marie-Laure. 2014. 'Story/Worlds/Media: Tuning the Instruments of a Media-Conscious Narratology,' in *Storyworlds Across Media: Toward a Media-Conscious Narratology*, edited by Marie-Laure Ryan and Jan-Noël Thon, pp. 25–49. Lincoln, NE: University of Nebraska Press.

Schackman, Daniel. 2013. 'Social Media Content,' in *The Social Media Industries*, edited by Alan B. Albarran, pp. 105–116. London: Routledge.

Scolari, Carlos A., Guerrero-Pico, Mar, and Establés, María-José. 2018. 'Spain: Emergences, Strategies and Limitations of Spanish Transmedia Productions,' in *Global Convergence Cultures: Transmedia Earth*, edited by Matthew Freeman and William Proctor, pp. 38–55. London: Routledge.

Wagner, Rachel. 2012. *Godwired: Religion, Ritual and Virtual Reality*. London: Routledge.

Yinger, J. Milton. 1970. *The Scientific Study of Religion*. London: Collier-Macmillan.

4 Mobile Games
Philosophical World-building

As part of the official press release for the announcement of a new virtual reality (VR) game based on the world of *The Walking Dead*, President of Skybound Interactive Dan Murray declared:

> *The Walking Dead*, it all comes back to moral choice and what would you do as the player. That's sort of the essential principal pillar of the IP. I think that's why people either read the comic, watch the show, or play the games . . . What better way to experience that than being in the environment itself?
>
> (Schwartz, 2017)

In response to this announcement, *IGN* reporter Terri Schwartz (2017) explained further how 'the focus of the VR game will be an immersive narrative storytelling experience that forces players to make the same complex moral choices faced with characters in other *Walking Dead* stories.' Far from 'a straight up horror VR game,' the *Walking Dead* VR game was instead to be about 'choice and discovery, along with the interaction implications [that] player decisions will have' (Schwartz, 2017). In effect, then, the ethos of the *Walking Dead* VR game – at least if its promotional paratexts are to be believed – is firmly rooted in the bringing together of VR gaming technology with themes associated with moral philosophy.

This chapter will explore the world-building practices that have been employed in and across a range of *The Walking Dead*'s other mobile gaming platforms. I argue that interactive mobile- and game-based technologies present new opportunities for what I call *philosophical world-building* on account of the degree of personal-ized moral choice and ontological ambiguity that such technologies afford. With Chapter 3 uniting its analyses of technological affor-dances with the behaviors of audiences, showing how social media platforms allow audiences to cross the line between real and imagi-nary, this chapter moves on to interrogate this kind of ontological theme even further. As will be demonstrated to various extents via Telltale Games' *The Walking Dead: The Game* (2012), *The Walking Dead: No Man's Land* (2015) mobile game, and *The Walking Dead: Our World* (2018) augmented reality (AR) game, given the way in which interactive choice operates in relation to the physical loca-tion of the user, i.e. in the context of often real-world surroundings, these games offer interactive philosophical experiences whose moral choices are given greater weight on account of their perceived proximity to the real world. Drawing on concepts from the field of philosophy, this chapter considers how these three mobile games each build the world of *The Walking Dead* by populating it with what Ryan calls *existents*, i.e. the characters that have special signifi-cance for the plot, and with *settings*, i.e. the spaces within which the existents are located, which in Ryan's work is used in a cognitive or ontological way to focus on storyworlds as imaginative experiences:

> In the case of fiction, this experience is a blend of knowledge and make-believe; the user who is immersed in a storyworld knows that it is created by the medium, but he or she pretends to be believe that it exists autonomously or, in other words, that it is real.
>
> (Ryan, 2014: 34–35)

In some ways, Ryan's characterization of existents and how audiences engage with them is itself rather philosophical by nature, hinting at questions of ontology and to what extent audiences may choose to perceive a fictional character as real or make-believe. How, though, do interactive media forms like mobile games, especially those ampli-fied via immersive AR technology – blending make-believe with the knowledge of reality via the affordances of such technology – shape world-building dynamics in the world of *The Walking Dead*? As will be analyzed via the three aforementioned mobile games, these texts each offer unique philosophical experiences whose world-building practices are underpinned by the degree of interactivity that in turn produces transmedia experiences based on choice.

Conceptualizing Mobile Media

Before analyzing the specifics of *The Walking Dead*'s mobile games and their attempts at what I describe as philosophical world-building via the likes of 'point-and-click' narratives as well as locative AR technologies, I will begin this chapter by first outlining some of the key theoretical pillars needed to conceptualize transmedia world-building as a mobile-based phenomenon. This means delving into existing scholarly understandings of mobile media and its related conceptions of interactivity, locative media, and, indeed, AR.

As seen in the previous two chapters, there is little doubt that digital technologies have caused a shift in user behavior, to such an extent that they are 'a part of life' (Belk, 2013: 477). Mobile devices came into play as they extended past telecommunications and integrated text messaging technologies into their media systems, which then led to further technological innovations as well as interactive and commercial possibilities (Goggin and Hjorth, 2009). Mobiles have become an important center of media and technological convergence (Jenkins, 2006) or of 'multimediality' by combining various 'media forms, channels and delivery systems' into a single platform (Oksman, 2009: 118), turning mobiles themselves into vessels for interactive media products (Goggin and Hjorth, 2009).

Technologists would describe the concept of interactivity in connection with computer and mobile applications or its features, while advertisers are mainly concerned with the way in which interactivity as a technology can 'add value to the communication process' (Johnson et al., 2006: 35–36), rather than with how it is actually conceptualized. For example, interactive VR technology has been used previously as part of the marketing for *The Walking Dead* television series: to promote the premiere episode from Season 8 the AMC VR app provided audiences with supplementary material, including an extended bonus scene from the premiere episode (Oh, 2017). Beyond being a marketing ploy, however, interactivity can be seen as an official characteristic of a media technology, one that is measured by the extent to which a medium can potentially allow users to exercise control on the 'content and/or form of the mediated communication' (Jensen and Toscan, 1999, cited in Mechant and Van Looy, 2014: 303), as will be explored soon via Telltale Games' *The Walking Dead: The Game*. And that degree of control over content brings with it certain philosophical questions to do with choice and power. In other words, interactivity – particularly more heightened interactive technologies such as the aforementioned VR app – itself exists on a continuum, with degrees of choice lessening or increasing depending on the platform and its interactive affordances.

Jensen broke this continuum down into several dimensions based on different 'communication patterns'; namely, whether interactivity constitutes a list of options of pre-produced/accessible information or content to choose from, whether it allows the user to generate content by inputting their own data into a system, and whether it can sense and 'register information' from users and then 'adapt and/or respond' to what the user wants or does, sometimes automatically (Jensen, 1998: 200). Jensen's taxonomy of interactive media will be explored in relation to the world-building dynamics of all three of this chapter's mobile games shortly, but for now it is important to highlight that digital interactivity has a social and even philosophical dimension to it, with Mechant and Van Looy (2014: 303) describing this dimension as 'a form of information exchange between different actors,' whether it be human to human or human to machines. This social dimension to interactivity will be important to analyzing *The Walking Dead*'s mobile-based philosophical world-building shortly.

As interactivity plays such a huge role in making new media attractive and beneficial to active audiences, it also impacts the range of new digital technologies that have crossed over onto mobile media platforms, including virtual and augmented realities, which themselves belong to the broader concept of 'extended reality' – a term referring to all combined real-and-virtual environments, typically generated by digital technology. Characteristically, the term 'extended realty' is a superset which includes the entire spectrum from 'the complete real' to 'the complete virtual' as laid out in Paul Milgram's reality–virtuality continuum (1994). In other words, extended reality encompasses all possible variations and compositions of real and virtual objects. And for that reason, the concept provides a highly useful approach to the classification of imaginary worlds, especially when mapped according to the specific affordances of, say, VR or AR.

VR, termed by and originated from Jaron Lanier while working on 'simulation projects' and 'virtual environments' in the 1980s, is most commonly known as an ideational computer-generated environment that allows users to have realistic interactions with it through the use of supporting equipment, namely VR headsets and sensory gloves (Hillis, 2014: 512). Meanwhile, AR, refers to the technologies that allow 'digital information' or virtual objects, i.e. two- and three-dimensional images, to interact with and merge or overlap with real-life environments (Bolter, 2014: 30). Paul Milgram (1994) posited that virtuality itself exists on a continuum, with one end of the spectrum consisting entirely of 'real objects' and surroundings (real environment) and the other end being completely virtual and synthetic (virtual environment), while other VR-related technologies lie in the middle, consisting of a blend of real and virtual spaces. AR falls under that category but leans closer towards the real environment as the user's perception comprises more of the physical world than the virtual world (Bolter, 2014: 30). Once used solely in lab research, AR has since been repurposed for commercial and entertainment purposes on account of the rise of mobile devices, particularly the smartphone (Bolter, 2014). Today, there are many mobile apps that utilize this technology for gaming purposes, such as *The Walking Dead: Our World*.

Generally, AR is divided into two types, one being 'location-aware' and the other being 'vision-based' (Petrucco and Agostini, 2016: 116). Location-aware AR connects with a device's GPS and adjusts its information presentation according to a user's location. Examples include apps such as Waze and Google Maps. Vision-based AR, meanwhile, displays virtual artifacts and information (or graphics) once a user aims their mobile device's camera at an object, such as the Snow App, Snapchat, and indeed *The Walking Dead: Our World* app-based game (Petrucco and Agostini, 2016). Snapchat's explosive popularity, of course – with users enjoying interacting with quirky animated camera lenses – has prompted the company to roll out new forms of mobile media advertising based on this technology. Still, beyond forms of advertising and hype-building, how can the use of AR technology on mobile devices be understood as a philosophically minded strategy for building existents and settings?

Engaging with such a question first means considering the role of locative media in today's media landscape. As hinted above, the way in which the likes of AR bring the perception of mobile screens and the real world closer together raises interesting questions about how users impart the weight on their own moral choices onto the imaginary world of the screen. The term 'locative media' was coined by Karlis Kalnins in 2003 (see Hemment, 2006), and is closely related to AR. But whereas the latter may have a large number of functions depending on the creator, the former concentrates mostly on social interaction with a place and with technology. Insofar as locative media projects have a social or personal background, they can encourage new ways of engaging with the layered histories, meanings, and sensory experiences of landscape. By way of example, Soundlines was a locative media project carried out with school children by Strata Collective, a group of artists working with story, music, and new media to create innovative learning experiences. The project involved field trips and pervasive media technology – and specialist training for the children in film, animation, music, and mediascape – where media becomes layered into the landscape, itself triggered by GPS when walking with headphones and portable computers.

At a time when audiences are said to be losing touch with their sense of place on account of the 'traditionally interlocking components of "place"' now being absorbed by the digital interfaces of mobile media (Meyrowitz, 1999: 100), the aforementioned conceptions of interactivity, extended reality, and locative mobile media all serve as the theoretical groundwork for understanding how such conceptions inform a mode of philosophical world-building. Jenkins famously argued that transmedia storytelling is 'the art of world-building' (2006: 166) – immersing audiences in a storyworld – but in straddling the boundaries between real-world environments and digital media interfaces, I will now explore how mobile-based gaming technologies open up world-building to philosophical dimensions.

The Walking Dead: The Game

There is, of course, a kind of inherent link between gaming and philosophy: both of these concepts are about subjectivity and experience, something that is only augmented in a transmedia context. For Helen W. Kennedy (2018: 74), indeed, 'the notion of *transmedia play* relates to the subjective position and experience of the audience member (player),' thus 'shifting the focus from the text itself to the manifesting game form or the game mechanic that is being generated for the newly configured audience – the player' (Kennedy, 2018: 72). Fittingly, the best way to illustrate a complicated philosophical concept is by framing it as a story or a game-like situation. Throughout this chapter I will turn to three seminal philosophical thought experiments so to demonstrate how the affordances of the three studied mobile games in this chapter each build the world of *The Walking Dead*, populating it with aspects relating to existents or settings. As we shall see, the world-creation value of *The Walking Dead: The Game* lies in terms of how it builds its settings, while the soon-to-be-discussed *The Walking Dead: No Man's Land* mobile game contributes most strikingly to the storyworld's existents. *The Walking Dead: Our World* AR game, meanwhile, contributes to both. The first of this chapter's three philosophical thought experiments is called Mary the Colorblind Neuroscientist, which is useful for characterizing the world-creation value of *The Walking Dead: The Game*, in particular. Mary the Colorblind Neuroscientist (sometimes referred to as the Inverted Spectrum Problem), tries to demonstrate that there are non-physical properties – and thus attainable knowledge – that can only be learned through conscious experience. The originator of the concept, Frank Jackson (1986: 292), explains it thusly:

Mary is a brilliant scientist who is, for whatever reason, forced to investigate the world from a black and white room via a black and white television monitor. She specializes in the neurophysiology of vision and acquires, let us suppose, all the physical information there is to obtain about what goes on when we see ripe tomatoes, or the sky, and use terms like 'red,' 'blue,' and so on. She discovers, for example, just which wavelength combinations from the sky stimulate the retina, and exactly how this produces via the central nervous system the contraction of the vocal cords and expulsion of air from the lungs that results in the uttering of the sentence 'The sky is blue.' What, though, will happen when Mary is released from her black and white room or is given a color television monitor? Will she learn anything new?

Put another way, Mary knows everything there is to know about color except for one crucial thing: she has never actually experienced color consciously. Her first experience of color was something that she could not possibly have anticipated; there is, the thought experiment posits, an important difference between academically knowing something versus having actual experience of that thing. This thought experiment teaches us that there will always be more to our perception of reality, including consciousness itself, than objective observation. Mary the Colorblind Neuroscientist shows us that we do not know what we do not know. In other words, it implies that we should all augment our sensory capabilities and our conscious awareness, opening up entirely new avenues of psychological and subjective exploration.

So, when applying Jackson's concept to the aims of this chapter, the most obvious question is: if television viewing versus gaming represents the proverbial difference between academically knowing something, i.e. passively watching a story event unfold, and having actual experience of that thing, i.e. interacting with it firsthand via gameplay, then what can only be learned about the world of *The Walking Dead* through conscious experience? How do the affordances of *The Walking Dead: The Game* allow users to learn something new?

The Walking Dead: The Game (also known as *The Walking Dead: Season One*) was the first in a series of episodic games developed and published by Telltale Games. Released between April and November 2012, the game was released on console platforms like Xbox 360 and PlayStation 4 as well as made available on mobile devices via Android and iOS. The story of the game takes place shortly after the onset of the zombie apocalypse in Georgia; most of the characters are original to the game, revolving for the most part around university professor and convicted criminal Lee Everett, who helps to rescue and subsequently care for a young girl named Clementine. Going back to Jensen's taxonomy of interactive media, *The Walking Dead: The Game* would therefore exemplify only the lowest point of this taxonomy, with interactivity constituting a list of options of pre-produced/accessible information or content to choose from (Jensen, 1998: 200). The game's point-and-click-style narratives are affected by both the dialogue choices of the user and their actions during quick-time events, which may lead to, for example, certain characters being killed or to an adverse change in the disposition of a certain character towards Lee. The choices made by the user carry over from episode to episode, with choices tracked by Telltale so to inform the writing of later episodes.

While *The Walking Dead: The Game* is thus not in any way an example of extended reality, which by definition encompasses combined variations of real and virtual objects, this game does nevertheless raise a set of philosophical questions about the relationship between fantasy and reality, and between make-believe and knowledge, in the world of *The Walking Dead*. Even on the most basic of levels, one can talk about the virtuality of imaginary worlds as often being inspired by the real world. According to Wolf (2017: 67), for instance, 'practically all imaginary worlds begin with the template of the Primary World, the world we live in, gradually replacing its default assumptions and structures with invented material.' For Wolf:

> this is necessary if the new secondary world is to be recognized as a world, and . . . we will project upon the [secondary world] everything we know about the real world . . . a gap-filling process that has been referred to by Kendall Walton (1990) as the 'reality principle' while Marie-Laure Ryan (1980) calls it the 'principle of minimal departure.'
>
> (Wolf, 2017: 67)

While some stories are content to be set in the Primary World, in existing cities, towns, and countries of the real world, even a single, profound difference can generate a very different storyworld. For example, in the first issue of *The Walking Dead* comic book, the story is set in the real U.S. state of Georgia, but the world on display has been overrun by hordes of zombies. In other words, and as Wolf's work would observe, the world of *The Walking Dead* is itself already very closely related to the real world, which is perhaps why it leaves itself so open to influence from real-world disciplinary approaches such as anthropology, sociology, religious studies, and, indeed, philosophy. Moreover, the world-creation value of the ability to exercise some degree of control over the game's mediated communication, i.e. the capacity to learn something new about the storyworld via conscious experience, is based on the game's capacity to heighten the user's emotional understanding of how living in the world of *The Walking Dead* would impact their own ability to live in and perceive the storyworld.

Allow me to demonstrate what I mean. In Episode 1, 'A New Day,' *The Walking Dead: The Game* opens with an establishing shot of a deserted Georgia freeway, the same deserted freeway that Rick rode down on a horse in both the comics and the television series. The game thus immediately 'diegetically braids' itself with that of the larger storyworld; that is to say, it connects itself with 'multiple stories . . . set in the same world' via the sharing of the same locations (Wolf, 2012: 376). That this same location happens to be the real place of Georgia only works to ground the game's ensuing moral choices with greater weight. Unlike the two later games to be discussed in this chapter, which to varying extents position the user as a god watching over the world's settings, *The Walking Dead: The Game* casts the user as protagonist Lee Everett, embodying a kind of 'user-within-a-democracy' aesthetic. In this way, *The Walking Dead: The Game* is an example of what Helen W. Kennedy (2018: 72–73) describes as a 'typical transmedia game': 'The text/story/images and places of the film or the novel or the television show become "playable" and potentially navigable (or open to exploration), allowing for a different subjectivity and an alternate mode of engagement.'

As the user plays through the five episodes, the big moral choices come when they are required to choose how Lee responds to situations and what he says in conversations with his fellow survivors. Choices and dialogue pop up on screen with timers, and the user has mere seconds to pick exactly what they are going to do or say. In *The Walking Dead: The Game*, the user makes a choice, and the game moves on – adapting its story to each decision. Spaces become the parameters for moral choices. As *IGN* reviewer Greg Miller (2012) elaborates:

> You and I are tasked with the same goal of protecting Clementine, but the way we do it might be completely different. I might choose

to befriend someone you hate, and you might choose to leave someone I took. I might shoot my mouth off in anger, but you might keep your cool; either way, the group will remember that and the dynamic will change. The decisions you're making in the moment have ripples that go throughout the entire adventure.

For example, one of the first choices the user is faced with in Episode 1 is deciding whether to save Shawn, son of Hershel, or Duck, son of Kenny. They have both been attacked by zombies: one grabbing Shawn as he is pinned underneath a tractor and another clutching Duck's shirt as he is perched on top of a tractor. With the user forced into making an impossible choice, i.e. to choose between one life and the other, *The Walking Dead: The Game* foregrounds its world's settings as spaces whose seemingly everyday objects exist mainly as tools to enact murderous carnage. Making the conscious choice to save one life over another, and being forced to choose how the less fortunate life must die, the game encourages the user to reflect emotionally on what the world has become, echoing Chapter 2's discussion of the way in which *The Walking Dead: Red Machete* webseries opened up sociological questions to do with how characters reacted to their fictional environment and audiences reflected on the passing of time. As one fan, surveyed for this book, stated:

> The mechanic of choosing the outcomes of the certain events is simple. You just hit a button and your fate is sealed. But the weight of each decision makes those moments radiate with importance, although you may not always know immediately what the consequences of your choices are. This isn't a game where you choose to go right and you are safe or left and you are in the fight. It's a culmination of everything you have done, good or bad.

However, do remember that the game exemplifies only the low end of Jensen's taxonomy of interactive media; *The Walking Dead: The Game* tells the same overarching story for all users, taking players to roughly the same conclusion, but it allows the individual user to experience this overarching story in very different ways, enacting different choices. In other words, while the basic settings of the game will remain the same regardless of the individual choices made by the user, the *nature* of those settings, i.e. who shares them with you, how welcoming or hostile they become, when and how you must leave them, and so on, is predicated on conscious experience. As another surveyed fan put it: 'The game challenges you by creating tense and moody atmospheres where no one is safe, and happy endings are the province of fairy tales.' Jackson's earlier outlined thought experiment highlighted that Mary, trapped in a black-and-white room watching the world through a black-and-white television, academically knew everything there was to know about color except for what it was like to actually experience the sight of color. Meanwhile, as Miller (2012) describes it:

> *The Walking Dead: The Game* is like a coloring book: we each have the same black and white sketch, but it's up to us to fill it in as we see fit. The relationships I've built, the emotions I've felt, the choices I've made – that's what makes *The Walking Dead: The Game* so endearing.

Proverbially speaking, in other words, *The Walking Dead: The Game* not only allows users to experience color; its interactive affordances allow some degree of control over what those colors actually are, where they go, and how they are perceived. And in doing so, the game reinforces Jackson's thought experiment: by augmenting users' sensory capabilities and their conscious awareness of living in the world of *The Walking Dead*, it opens up new avenues of psychological and subjective exploration based on how it would feel, and indeed what it would take out of a person, to make the kinds of brutal choices necessary to survive in the spaces of this storyworld. Watching Rick massacre Gareth with the red machete in Season 5 of the television series allows us to observe the act of murder, but *The Walking Dead: The Game* forces us to experience the act of murder, for we do not know what we do not know.

The Walking Dead: No Man's Land

The theme of conscious experience is also important to *The Walking Dead: No Man's Land*, a mobile game produced by Next Games and launched on iOS and Android in 2015, albeit in a very different way.

Billed as 'The Official Mobile Game of AMC's *The Walking Dead*,'
The Walking Dead: No Man's Land is described as

> a thrilling, action-packed RPG where tactical choices make the dif-
> ference between life and death: bring Michonne and dominate in
> close-quarter combat or send Rick to dispatch enemies from afar.
> Or perhaps you'll choose to snipe from a distance with Daryl's
> crossbow, or mow the herd down with Abraham's assault rifle.

It is important to note that the game is listed on Google Play as a
'strategy' game, and one that allows users to make strategic decisions through the eyes of core characters: 'Play now with Daryl, Rick,
Michonne and many other characters of AMC's *The Walking Dead*!'

This emphasis on strategy and perspective is significant for our purposes, and allows us to turn to the discipline of philosophy – itself the
study of existence and reality – to make sense of the game-based building
of existents and settings in the world of *The Walking Dead*. In essence,
The Walking Dead: No Man's Land affords world-building, namely of
existents, via a shift in perspective and relationship between user and
character, with its interactive, strategic affordances allowing users both
to project their own ideas about characters and to gain unique access into
their minds, thus raising a set of interesting philosophical questions.

Understanding this approach to world-building means framing
our analysis once again via a philosophical thought experiment,
one that – on this occasion – considers the difficulties of knowing
an individual mind. Known as The Beetle in the Box, the concept
derives from Ludwig Wittgenstein's *Philosophical Investigations*
(1953), in which he proposed a thought experiment that challenged
the way we look at introspection and how it informs the language we
use to describe sensations. For this thought experiment, Wittgenstein
asks us to imagine a group of individuals, each of whom has a box
containing something called a 'beetle.' No one can see into anyone
else's box. Everyone is asked to describe their beetle but each person only knows their own beetle. Each person can only talk about
their own beetle, as there might be different things in each person's
box. Consequently, Wittgenstein says, people will talk about what
is in their boxes, but the word 'beetle' simply ends up meaning 'that
thing that is in a person's box.' Wittgenstein's thought experiment

points out that the 'beetle' is like our minds, i.e. something that can be described by others, though we cannot ever truly know what it is like in another individual's mind. It was a demonstration of the impossibility of ever knowing the unique perspective of another person's experience.

Wittgenstein's notion is true to a large extent, though it becomes problematized when the 'person' in question is one of fiction, and indeed when said fictional person is rendered via the mechanics of a mobile game. When watching a character such as Daryl on television, with the viewer a mere passive outsider to the make-believe of the storyworld, we may not ever truly know what it is like inside his mind. But in the context of *The Walking Dead: No Man's Land*, Daryl's mind opens up in a way largely unseen on television. Let's consider an example. At the very start of the game (Part 1, Episode 1: 'Road to Terminus') the user is merely following orders: characters Joel, Ken, and Ann are at the disposal of the user, who – taking orders from Daryl – must fight through a horde of zombies in Terminus. 'Clear this place of walkers and you'll have a place of your own,' instructs Daryl. 'Your turn. Kill the closest walkers.' In fact, voices of authority in the game typically come from established core characters from the television series, such as Daryl. Almost immediately, Daryl is the one who initiates the game's first mission, acting as the leader that directs the narrative for the user. 'We gotta go back to Terminus,' Daryl insists. 'I got you folks out but there may be more still locked up there. We can't just let them starve. We'll have to fight our way back.'

In effect, then, *The Walking Dead: No Man's Land* can be understood to build the character of Daryl in a unique way, demonstrating how he would behave if required to act as a leader of a group (a role that he is not needed to perform on television due to the centrality of Rick). Without the leadership of Rick at the start of the game, though, Daryl steps up, and the mobile game thus provides an insight into his strategic capabilities as a character: 'The road's swarming with walkers. We'll have to clear it in steps. Carry whatever you can find. This ain't the time to be fussy.' In other words, the affordances of *The Walking Dead: No Man's Land* work to allow audiences to know a different perspective of the character's mind, with the direct communicative relationship constructed between character and user echoing Ryan's assertion that audiences may well believe a storyworld and its characters to be real.

Indeed, the fact that the world of *The Walking Dead* is itself so intrinsically related to our own world, as noted earlier, only works to further autotomize these character traits as real.

As the game progresses, however, *The Walking Dead: No Man's Land* requires the user to become more and more of a leader. Tasks revolve around the user building a farm; populating it with training facilities; gathering food, weapons, and armor to survive; choosing the right team and equipment for missions; training characters to fight and gather supplies, and so on. In terms of Jensen's earlier outlined taxonomy of interactive media, *The Walking Dead: No Man's Land* thereby sits at the midpoint of this taxonomy: allowing the user to generate content by inputting their own data into a system (Jensen, 1998: 200). And this degree of interactivity transforms the philosophical dimensions of Wittgenstein's The Beetle in the Box thought experiment into something much more god-like in terms of character insight.

Indeed, *The Walking Dead: No Man's Land* adopts what might be described as a 'user-as-god aesthetic': the viewing angle is always from above looking down on the characters and action below. The game is predicated on the user effectively shepherding multiple characters along as a dictator, choosing their actions for them. This is different to the gaming experience of *The Walking Dead: The Game*, which was based on playing as one character, embodying a kind of 'user-within-a-democracy' aesthetic as the choices of the user impacted those around them. In one sense, therefore, the god's-eye-view aesthetic of this game reinforces the themes of dictatorship that were highlighted as narratively significant to the world of *The Walking Dead* in Chapter 1. But what does this god's-eye-view aesthetic, combined with this level of interactivity, mean to notions of world-building? In particular, how do the actions of the user – not playing as an individual character, but using and moving multiple characters strategically – contribute more knowledge about those characters?

Put simply, the answer to this question lies in the way that the strategic, god's-eye-view aesthetic of *The Walking Dead: No Man's Land* actually subverts character insight, allowing users to know some characters *less*. The user can choose how to build a community, when to radio for fellow survivors, when to bring those survivors into the group, how to use supplies, and so on. It is made clear within the narrative of the game that the user is the one making these choices for the various characters within the community; again, the user is the sole dictator making all decisions for everyone else. Philosophically speaking, in other words, and in ways that both echo and distort the religious world-building analyzed in the previous chapter, *The Walking Dead: No Man's Land* denies many of its characters the chance to even describe their proverbial beetle; instead, the user describes it for them, with said user projecting what they imagine – or perhaps what they themselves want or need – the minds of characters to be. As has been argued throughout this entire book, once again it therefore becomes the role of audiences to contribute to world-building phenomena via their own inner imaginations, memories, beliefs, and desires. In the specific case of *The Walking Dead: No Man's Land*, it may well be an impossibility to ever truly know the unique perspective of another person's mind or experience, as per Wittgenstein's thought experiment, but this particular mobile game trounces this philosophical problem of subjectivity by allowing users not to become the minds of characters, but rather to colonize those minds in ways that become useful for the whims of the user, building up expectations for how existents should think and act in the world of *The Walking Dead*. Such an imposing God-like philosophy to existents may go against the more collective religious world-building of Chapter 3, but it is perfectly in line with many views held within the storyworld. Midway through Season 2 of *Fear the Walking Dead*, for example, Travis and his son Chris (Lorenzo James Henrie) are traveling the Mexican border when they run into a group of American students. One of the students, relishing the freedom of living in a zombie apocalypse, explains his euphoric philosophy on the new world to Travis:

> We got no speed limits, no cops, no money, no work, no bills, no bullshit. We're just living. It's more than living – it's supernatural. We were nothing before this, man. We were less than. But now? The end times made us *Gods*.

The Walking Dead: Our World

This kind of overt god-like philosophy to the shaping of existents across media has further implications when considered in the context of more immersive media technologies. One such example is *The*

Walking Dead: Our World, a location-based AR mobile game developed by Next Games and released in 2018. Sharing an element of the strategy focus that characterized *The Walking Dead: No Man's Land, The Walking Dead: Our World* is described on its official website as allowing users to 'explore and defend your neighborhood: Get out in the real world to move your avatar in the game . . . Collect stashes, find missions and rescue survivors with other players.' But the game's key selling feature is that it enables the user to 'immerse [themselves] in the zombie apocalypse by fighting off walkers in Augmented Reality!' What impact, however, do the affordances of locative gaming media, specifically AR technology, have on the building of existents and settings?

Specifically, understanding the world-creation value of AR technology in *The Walking Dead: Our World* means turning once again to a philosophical thought experiment. This time, I point to the renowned moral philosopher Philippa Foot. This thought experiment, of which there are now many variations, first appeared in Foot's 1967 paper titled 'Abortion and the Doctrine of Double Effect.' Most colloquially, it is referred to as The Trolley Problem. Imagine that you are at the controls of a railway switch and there is an out-of-control trolley coming. The railway tracks soon branch into two: one track leads to a group of five people and the other to one person. If you do nothing, the trolley will smash into the five people. But if you flip the switch at the controls, the trolley will change tracks and strike the lone person. As one might expect, different philosophical groups have offered different perspectives on this issue. Utilitarians, who seek to maximize happiness, say that the single person should be killed. Kantians, meanwhile – because they see people as ends and not means – would argue that you cannot treat the single person as a means for the benefit of the five. Thus, you should do nothing. Above all, this thought experiment reveals the complexity of morality by distinguishing between the activity of killing a person and the passivity of letting them die, a problem that is further complicated by the affordances of AR technology.

Indeed, in terms of Jensen's aforementioned taxonomy of interactive media, *The Walking Dead: Our World* sits squarely at the highest point of this taxonomy: allowing the user to register information and then adapt and/or respond to what the user wants or does, sometimes automatically (Jensen, 1998: 200). The game draws on Google maps to allow users to take on missions in their own neighborhood, where a real-world map of a player's surroundings is transformed into a post-apocalyptic landscape riddled with supply crates, walker encounters, and user-built shelters that serve as drop off points for survivors. And this high degree of interactivity works to further heighten the philosophical dimensions of Foot's The Trolley Problem thought experiment into something that, in one sense, augments the world of *The Walking Dead*'s 'principle of minimal departure,' i.e. its already close relationship with the real world, while, in another sense, becomes even more philosophically problematic.

Indeed, *The Walking Dead: Our World*'s gameplay is dramatically enhanced by playing with a group. For example, joining an in-game group of survivors and core characters like Rick, Michonne, and Daryl gives users access to greater rewards and allows them to participate in 'Challenge Boards,' thus further extending the social rules and values to do with community that in Chapter 3 I argued became a kind of faith for the storyworld's fans via the affordances of social media platforms. But in another sense, the affordances of AR establish a series of interactive choices to do with killing that are presented in the context of the user's physical surroundings; that is to say, it makes the active choice of killing seem more real, with consequences that are implied even if they are not actualized within the game.

Much of these consequences stem from the visual style of the game itself. The combat style of *The Walking Dead: Our World* is a first-person shooting experience, with selectable (and discoverable) guns. This is where the AR part of *The Walking Dead: Our World* comes in. To use the AR in combat encounters, users tap an 'AR available' toggle and point their phones at the ground. If the conditions are right, returning the phone to a central position shows the user's selected character companion superimposed in their real world surroundings, with zombies lurking a few steps away. Foot's seminal thought experiment explored the complex morality of choosing between one life and another, distinguishing between the activity of killing one life and the passivity of letting multiple people die, an idea that was exemplified by *The Walking Dead: The Game*, where the user was often forced into making an impossible choice between saving one life over another. But the affordances of AR in *The Walking*

Dead: Our World actually work to achieve a different moral effect; that is, to distort the line between killing a single make-believe zombie and letting hordes of 'real' people die: the latter become a kind of collateral damage in the act of killing the former.

Here is an example. Alexis Nedd (2018), in her review of the game for Mashable UK, argued that, philosophically, the issue with using AR in a first-person shooter is that real people can walk into frame while players are mowing enemies down in the game: 'On a crowded city street, it can be hard to tell the visual difference between the moving body of a zombie and some random guy on his lunch break.' The experience of using AR to aim and shoot at real people, even if said real people are not the intended targets, is, Nedd (2018) continues, 'disturbing on its face and does not pass the "what's the worst thing someone can do with this technology" test that every developer should consider before releasing a game.' In many respects, *The Walking Dead: Our World* is the most interactively extreme exemplar of Ryan's phenomenological assertion that audiences may believe a storyworld to be real.

In effect, the use of AR in *The Walking Dead: Our World* is thus essentially about blurring the line between digital and real-world environments, between make-believe and real knowledge, by creating a world of extended reality. At any one moment, those engaging with *The Walking Dead: Our World* are experiencing the real world and the virtual world on top of each other, with mobile devices and AR drawing attention to the overlap between those worlds in ways that work to further reinforce the world of *The Walking Dead* as one very closely related to our own. In doing so, users are simultaneously drawn into the game's world by images, narratives, and interfaces of make-believe before being asked to perform the realities of violence in their own world. In that sense, *The Walking Dead: Our World* is a mobile game that encourages users not to escape from reality by entering a fictional storyworld – as one assumes to be the objective with most of the big transmedia properties now populating Hollywood and beyond – but rather to believe in the imaginary world as itself reality by traversing the line between real and virtual. It asks us to strip away any semblance of philosophical ambiguity over the act of killing; in this game, and indeed in this world, the philosophical dilemma of Foot's The Trolley Problem does not even apply. For the need to survive amidst the apocalypse means that there is no longer any difference between the activity of killing and the passivity of letting people die, just as the affordances of AR technology mean that there is no longer a difference between the real and the virtual.

And such a complex philosophy for how existents behave amidst the settings of the world of *The Walking Dead* – one that reinforces a god-like power for the user while also distorting the line between killing a single make-believe zombie and letting hordes of 'real' people die as collateral damage in the name of survival – is once again in line with that of the larger storyworld. Midway through Season 5 of the television series, for example, with Rick and his group at one of their lowest points – no home, no food, and hope running low after the recent death of Beth – they find temporary shelter in a barn as they wait out a major storm. In an effort to motivate the group to keep on fighting, Rick invoked the name of the series in a speech that, in many ways, epitomizes the philosophy of the entire storyworld:

> When I was a kid, I asked my grandpa once if he ever killed any Germans in the war. He wouldn't answer. He said that was grown-up stuff, so I asked if the Germans ever tried to kill him. But he got real quiet. He said he was dead the minute he stepped into enemy territory. Every day he woke up and told himself, 'Rest in peace. Now get up, and go to war.' And then after a few years of pretending he was dead, he made it out alive. That's the trick of it, I think. We do what we need to do, and then we get to live. But no matter what [happens], I know we'll be okay, because this is how we survive. We tell ourselves that *we* are the walking dead.

Conclusion

The growing use of mobile devices and smartphones may have allowed marketers and businesses more broadly to help them track, target, reach, and measure their online audiences and revenue, but the rapid advancements in mobile gaming technology have also provided numerous methods of engagement with audiences (Tuten, 2008: 9). This chapter, however, has begun to demonstrate the relationship between such rapid technological advancements in mobile gaming and world-building, stressing, once again, the importance of audiences. Raymond Williams (2003 [1974]: 4) once noted that 'we do not know, in any particular case, whether, for example, we are talking about a technology or about the uses of a technology; about a content or a form.' Just as Williams proposed a sort of combination of the two when thinking about the relationship between television and its audiences, i.e. a recognition of the 'known social needs, purposes and practices to which the technology is not marginal, but central' (Williams, 2003 [1974]: 8), this chapter has shown how making stories playable brings philosophical world-building opportunities based on 'situat[ing] the player behaviors and pleasures as dependent upon the subjectivities of a ludic cultural imaginary' (Kennedy, 2018: 80).

In the case of the world of *The Walking Dead*, and specifically with regards to *The Walking Dead: The Game, The Walking Dead: No Man's Land*, and *The Walking Dead: Our World*, one might observe how the spectrum of Jensen's taxonomy of interactivity gave way to a ludic cultural imaginary that reinforced the philosophy of the entire storyworld. Put simply, the higher up the spectrum of Jensen's taxonomy the game came to exemplify, the more it worked to embody the idea that existents have come to behave like gods amidst settings, no longer tied to or emotionally affected by the moral systems of the storyworld. I argued in Chapter 1 that the world of *The Walking Dead* is populated with characters who are essentially stripped of their histories; the shift from a 'user-within-a-democracy' aesthetic in *The Walking Dead: The Game* to a 'user-as-god aesthetic' in *The Walking Dead: No Man's Land*, and finally to a fully-blended extended reality aesthetic in *The Walking Dead: Our World*, is representative of how engaging in transmedia activities can transform the person as much as the storyworld. For those users who progressively consumed all three games as they were released, then, their own moral journey across these three games may well have come to mirror that of Rick's moral journey and his aforementioned philosophy that surviving in this storyworld means believing that you are dead, that you yourself are the walking dead.

And transmediality, with its innate power to immerse users in interactive practices and shared, connected experiences, is fundamental to this kind of world-creation. For as Nataly Rios Gioco (2018: 478) argues,

> one of the things about transmedia is that it allows you to associate virtual spaces and real spaces with a story . . . . Through transmedia we can expand the experience of the real world to the digital world, and vice versa.

Opening up analyses of the world-creation value of mobile gaming to the discipline of philosophy thus enables researchers to explore how transmedia experiences across actual and virtual terrains actively encourage audiences to question their own subjective experience of a storyworld. I have shown how three philosophical thought experiments become useful analytic tools for describing a philosophical form of world-building. This approach emphasizes the building of imaginary worlds as a process of experiential engagement based on choice and consequence.

References

Belk, Russell W. 2013. 'Extended Self in a Digital World,' *Journal of Consumer Research* 40: 477–500.

Bolter, Jay David. 2014. 'Augmented Reality,' in *The Johns Hopkins Guide to Digital Media*, edited by Marie-Laure Ryan, Lori Emerson, and Benjamin J. Robertson, pp. 30–32. Baltimore, MD: Johns Hopkins University Press.

Foot, Philippa. 1967. 'Abortion and the Doctrine of Double Effect,' *Oxford Review* 5: 21–29.

Gioco, Nataly Rios. 2018. 'Afterword: The Present and Future of Transmedia Practices – A Conversation,' in *The Routledge Companion to Transmedia Studies*, edited by Matthew Freeman and Renira Rampazzo Gambarato, pp. 473–480. London: Routledge.

Goggin, Gerrard and Hjorth, Larissa. 2009. 'The Question of Mobile Media,' in *Mobile Technologies: From Telecommunications to Media*, edited by Gerard Goggin and Larissa Hjorth, pp. 3–8. London: Routledge.

Hemment, Drew. 2006. 'Locative Arts,' *Leonardo* 39(4): 348–355.

Hillis, Ken. 2014. 'Virtual Reality,' in *The Johns Hopkins Guide to Digital Media*, edited by Marie-Laure Ryan, Lori Emerson, and Benjamin J. Robertson, pp. 510–514. Baltimore, MD: Johns Hopkins University Press.

Jackson, Frank. 1986. 'What Mary Didn't Know,' *The Journal of Philosophy* 83(5): 291–295.

Jenkins, Henry. 2006. *Convergence Culture: Where Old and New Media Collide*. New York: New York University Press.

Jensen, Jens F. 1998. 'Interactivity: Tracking a New Concept in Media and Communication Studies,' *NORDICOM Review* 19(1): 185–204.

Johnson, James, Bruner II, Gordon C., and Kumar, Anand. 2006. 'Interactivity and Its Facets Revisited: Theory and Empirical Test,' *Journal of Advertising* 35(4): 35–52.

Kennedy, Helen W. 2018. 'Transmedia Games: Aesthetics and Politics of Profitable Play,' in *The Routledge Companion to Transmedia Studies*, edited by Matthew Freeman and Renira Rampazzo Gambarato, pp. 72–81. London: Routledge.

Mechant, Peter and Van Looy, Jan. 2014. 'Interactivity,' in *The Johns Hopkins Guide to Digital Media*, edited by Marie-Laure Ryan, Lori Emerson, and Benjamin J. Robertson, pp. 302–305. Baltimore, MD: Johns Hopkins University Press.

Meyrowitz, Joshua. 1999. 'No Sense of Place: The Impact of Electronic Media on Social Behavior,' in *The Media Reader: Continuity and Transformation*, edited by Hugh Mackay and Tim O'Sullivan, pp. 99–120. London: SAGE Publications.

Milgram, Paul. 1994. 'A Taxonomy of Mixed Reality Visual Displays,' *IEICE Transactions on Information and Systems* 12: 1321–1329.

Miller, Greg. 2012. 'The Walking Dead: The Game Review,' *IGN.com* (December 12). http://uk.ign.com/articles/2012/12/12/the-walking-dead-the-game-review (accessed August 26, 2018).

Nedd, Alexis. 2018. 'New Walking Dead Mobile Game Has a Killer Social Element, But Fairly Pointless AR,' *Mashable.com*. (July 21). https://mashable.com/2018/07/21/the-walking-dead-our-world-ar-game-review/?europe=true (Accessed August 28, 2018).

Oh, Sheryl. 2017. 'AMC's VR App Brings New Immersive Content From The Walking Dead,' *Filmschoolrejects.com* (October 20). https://filmschoolrejects.com/amc-vr-app-brings-new-immersive-content-walking-dead/ (accessed August 2, 2018).

Oksman, Virpi. 2009. 'Media Contents in Mobiles: Comparing Video, Audio, and Text,' in *Mobile Technologies: From Telecommunications to Media*, edited by Gerard Goggin and Larissa Hjorth, pp. 118–130. London: Routledge.

Petrucco, Corrado, and Agostini, Daniele. 2016. 'Teaching Our Cultural Heritage Using Mobile Augmented Reality,' *Journal of E-Learning & Knowledge Society* 12(3): 115–128.

Ryan, Marie-Laure. 1980. 'Fiction, Non-Factuals and the Principle of Minimal Departure,' *Poetics* 8: 403–422.

Ryan, Marie-Laure. 2014. 'Story/Worlds/Media: Tuning the Instruments of a Media-Conscious Narratology,' in *Storyworlds Across Media: Toward a*

Media-Conscious Narratology, edited by Marie-Laure Ryan and Jan-Noël Thon, pp. 25–49. Lincoln, NE: University of Nebraska Press.

Schwartz, Terri. 2017. 'The Walking Dead Is Coming to VR in Multiple New Games,' *IGN.com* (June 14). http://uk.ign.com/articles/2017/06/14/e3-2017-the-walking-dead-is-coming-to-vr-in-multiple-new-games (accessed July 23, 2018).

Tuten, Tracy L. 2008. *Advertising 2.0: Social Media Marketing in a Web 2.0 World.* Westport, CT: Praeger Publishing.

Walton, Kendall. 1990. *Mimesis as Make-Believe: On the Foundations of Representational Arts.* Cambridge, MA: Harvard University Press.

Williams, Raymond. 2003 [1974]. *Television: Technology and Cultural Form.* London: Routledge.

Wittgenstein, Ludwig. 2009 [1953]. *Philosophical Investigations.* Hoboken, NJ: Wiley-Blackwell.

Wolf, Mark J.P. 2012. *Building Imaginary Worlds: The Theory and History of Subcreation.* London: Routledge.

Wolf, Mark J.P. (ed.) 2017. *The Routledge Companion to Imaginary Worlds.* London: Routledge.

Conclusion
Towards a Transdisciplinary World-building Framework

In a media landscape marked by the often opposing forces of media consolidation and audience fragmentation, *The Walking Dead* – a storyworld with a relatively longstanding top-tier cultural status whose audiences are nevertheless scattered and splintered in and across a range of platforms – typifies the challenges currently faced for researchers when attempting to analyze with any degree of rigor how the pieces of an imaginary world fit together. Yet at a time when many scholars seem preoccupied with the fading borders between different media platforms, this book has delved into the kinds of unique world-building trends that emerge from comics, television, social media, and mobile games, tracing how particular affordances of platform or technology lead to specific opportunities to build imaginary worlds. But as I have also argued elsewhere, 'to understand what transmediality really means, we have to talk more about navigation, and in particular the ways in which people move across physical and virtual spheres, and what motivates that process of moving. This means analyzing the behaviors and motivations of a media-crossing audience with much more rigor' (Freeman and Gambarato, 2018: 9), assessing the particularities of how an audience chooses (or chooses not) to migrate across media when engaging with a given imaginary world. In effect, it is my hope that the combined transdisciplinary and transmedial approach of this book will allow us as scholars to move beyond assumptions that 'media worlds could and should be somewhat inhabitable' (Gray, 2010: 187), and instead to more fully interrogate how the practices of both building and consuming imaginary worlds open up understandings of historiography, social relationships, beliefs, and philosophies, and indeed vice versa.

As such, it is certainly important to begin theorizing different conceptual models for how we study the ways that fans traverse media platforms in the context of world-building. For as William Proctor (2018: 116) notes, 'worldbuilding can sometimes be quite messy and knotted, *contra* utopian transmedia storytelling.' In the Introduction to this book I began to explain the limits of analyzing the world of *The Walking Dead* through the lens of media and literary studies concepts, such as paratext and possible worlds theory. How, though, has a transdisciplinary approach to studying this world enabled me to assess how the pieces of this imaginary world fit together (or contradict each other), which ones presuppose each other, which ones are self-sufficient and which ones are not, and which patterns of use dominate?

I have argued that taking a deliberately transdisciplinary approach to the study of the world of *The Walking Dead*, engaging with a far wider pool of disciplinary perspectives and concepts drawn from the fields of history, sociology, anthropology, religious studies, and philosophy, has led to an understanding of this particular storyworld as a place that is not constructed or indeed consumed as any kind of absolute. Rather, the world of *The Walking Dead* is a reflection of, on the one hand, the storyworld's inherent sense of discrepancy and subjectivity, denied as it is the possibility of a single, standardized chronicle of its own events on account of the downfall of the society it depicts, a world with no government, no media, and thus no objective, overarching narrative about what is happening in the world or why. And hence, on the other hand, the world of *The Walking Dead* is equally a reflection of its audience's preferences for particular sets of platforms and their own broader media habits, daily routines, and ideologies, guided by the changing interpretations of the world's events.

The journey of the book can be summarized thusly: Chapter 1 dealt with how the core pieces of the world of *The Walking Dead* fit together via individual behavioral patterns and preferences; Chapter 2 looked at how individual emotional reactions are orchestrated and expanded across different digital terrains; Chapter 3 explored how individuals come together as a community to clarify complex moral questions about the storyworld; and Chapter 4 dealt with how the moral philosophy of the storyworld becomes redefined by interactive choice. In other words, *subjectivity* is critical to answering the central questions of this book. As has been argued throughout all four chapters, audiences contribute to world-building phenomena via their behaviors, emotions, beliefs, and choices, with these personal attributes shaping where they go next in the storyworld, which itself is shaped by their broader media routines. It has therefore been crucial to analyze manifestations of the world of *The Walking Dead* that span what I characterized in Chapter 3 as 'into the scenes' (diegetic) and 'behind the scenes' (extra-diegetic). To paraphrase the Aristotelian narrative distinction described in Chapter 1, there is a difference between the storyworld that is *told* and the storyworld that is *lived*.

From Hyper-diegetic Storyworlds to Intra-textual Storyworlds

Allow me to explain what I mean by the above Aristotelian narrative distinction, which I will elaborate upon in the aim of establishing at least the beginnings of a more transdisciplinary framework for analyzing imaginary worlds. If a perspective based on the storyworld that is *told* involves analysis of the media itself and how it depicts an imaginary world, perhaps via a semiotic or brand perspective for example, then a perspective based on the storyworld that is *lived* would place emphasis on what an imaginary world means to its audiences, perhaps looking at how they interact with it, when, and why. In effect, taking a transdisciplinary approach to the world of *The Walking Dead* has allowed me to combine these perspectives.

Indeed, while many studies of world-building tend to consider these processes from largely a narrative-centric perspective (hence the kinds of issues to do with canonicity and compossibility outlined in the introduction), this book has been much more interested in the expansion of world-based *mythology*, exploring this as a process based on a combination of technological affordances and audience dynamics; or, as Boothe (2018: 61) described it, 'the techno-social development of digital media and the sociocultural development of fan studies.' In short, this book has dealt with the far less tangible modes of world-building, exploring the ways in which an imaginary world can shape, interlace with, and even inspire our daily behaviors, emotions, beliefs, and choices, and arguing that the act of engaging with transmedia activities can profoundly transform the person as much as the storyworld.

Thinking about the world-creation value of such less tangible modes of world-building means thinking beyond what Matt Hills (2002: 137) calls the 'hyperdiegesis,' 'the creation of a vast and detailed narrative space, only a fraction of which is ever directly seen or encountered within the text, but which nonetheless appears to operate according to principles of internal logic and extension.' A hyperdiegesis may evoke the presence of a larger spatial structure in a storyworld, supporting an infinite amount of plots and characters, but this concept does little to accommodate the world-creation value of the sorts of highly subjective audience behaviors, emotions, beliefs, and choices discussed in this book.

A transdisciplinary framework for analyzing imaginary worlds would thus see the transmediation between the different platforms as a network of interlaced yet often highly subjective behaviors, emotions, beliefs, and choices – held together by what Boothe (2018: 67) refers to as 'intra-textuality.' For Boothe (2018: 67), 'this intra-textual force is reliant on the influences of audiences and fans, bringing an interactive element to the intertextual connections.' As has been demonstrated in numerous ways throughout the pages of this book, technological affordances – be them for web-series, interactive apps, chat shows, social media sites, or mobile games – each work to shape and inspire the behaviors, emotions, beliefs, and choices of audiences in often very specific ways, with both of these techno-social and sociocultural perspectives informing and expanding the mythology of a given storyworld.

Let's, then, try and be a bit more specific about how these ideas play out in practice. As per Chapter 1, to understand behavioral patterns of how audiences engage with and shape imaginary world mythology as part of their daily lives, one would be wise to make use of historiographical concepts and approaches, mapping how the affordances of a technology or platform work in dialogue with (or sometimes oppose) the relative practices and preferences of audiences. Historiographical world-building is all about how audiences *behave*, analyzing how fans may wish to exchange different, often conflicting interpretations of a storyworld. This approach revels in the multiplicity by which a world's meaning may operate in culture according to a particular set of contexts, such as a specific platform, and allows the researcher to make sense of how the meaning in one media site is defined by its relationship to other instances, both past, to which it responds, and future, whose response it anticipates.

Meanwhile, and as per Chapter 2, to understand emotional patterns of how audiences engage with and shape imaginary world mythology as part of their daily lives, one would be wise to make use of sociological concepts and approaches, in this case mapping the relationship between the affordances of a technology or platform and how audiences react. Sociological world-building is about how audiences *feel* – for as I argued in Chapter 2, it is not just a narrative that is constructed across different media, but equally the emotional fallout of audiences, building opportunities for catharsis, closure, reflection, reaction, and so on, quite often via the temporally arranged juxtaposition from one medium to another.

By comparison, and as per Chapter 3, to understand patterns of belief in terms of how an audience engages with and shapes imaginary world mythology as part of daily life, one should turn to concepts and approaches from religious studies, mapping how the affordances of a technology or platform initiate the kinds of belief systems that audiences hold in relation to a storyworld. Religious world-building is about what audiences *believe*, analyzing, on the one hand, the mutual relationships between an audience's curation, aggregation, and collaboration practices and how these work to embed a set of fictional belief systems into daily life, and, on the other hand, the impact of these belief systems on the storyworld itself.

Lastly, and as per Chapter 4, to understand patterns of choice in terms of how audiences engage with and shape imaginary world mythology as part of their daily lives, one would be wise to make use of philosophical concepts and approaches, in this case mapping the relationship between the affordances of a technology or platform and how audiences think. Philosophical world-building is about what audiences *choose* to do, and what they *think* about that choice. In the context of engaging with imaginary worlds, a philosophical approach would prioritize understanding the meaning of a subjective experience of a given storyworld, engaging, in particular, with the world-creation value of interactive choices.

Naturally, a transdisciplinary framework for analyzing world-building would be only enhanced by considering a far broader number of disciplines than I have suggested here. This book may have opted to focus primarily on historiography, sociology, anthropology, religious studies, and philosophy, but there is little doubt that the sub-field of imaginary world studies would be enriched greatly by an even wider pool of disciplinary perspectives. For instance, I am sure that the field of physics, focused as it is around questions of parallel universes and black holes, has much more to say about the creation processes of imaginary worlds (see Ryan, 2006). For now, though, a key takeaway from this book must be the value of seeing world-building as an innately *social* phenomenon. Chapter 2 may have explicitly engaged with the discipline of sociology and its focus on human experience, but the idea of religion that underpinned Chapter 3 was also based on a sociological perspective, as was the historiographical idea of polyglossia in Chapter 1 and the philosophical thought experiments that informed Chapter 4. In effect, all four of this book's chapters show vividly how important social dimensions have become to the workings of storyworlds, but also to communication and culture at large, given the shifts towards digital convergence and participatory media. All of this hints at the need to define imaginary worlds in sociological terms, by which I mean the role of imaginary worlds in helping us to better understand how we navigate daily life.

References

Boothe, Paul. 2018. 'Audience and Fan Studies: Technological Communities and Their Influences on Narrative Ecosystems,' in *Reading Contemporary Serial Television Universes: A Narrative Ecosystem Framework*, edited by Paola Brembilla and Ilaria A. De Pascalis, pp. 57–73. London: Routledge.

Freeman, Matthew and Gambarato, Renira Rampazzo. 2018. *The Routledge Companion to Transmedia Studies*. London: Routledge.

Gray, Jonathan. 2010. *Show Sold Separately: Promos, Spoilers, and Other Media Paratexts*. New York: New York University Press.

Hills, Matt. 2002. *Fan Cultures*. London: Routledge.

Proctor, William. 2018. 'United States: Trans-worldbuilding in the Stephen King Multiverse,' in *Global Convergence Cultures: Transmedia Earth*, edited by Matthew Freeman and William Proctor, pp. 101–120. London: Routledge.

Ryan, Marie-Laure. 2006. 'From Parallel Universes to Possible Worlds: Ontological Pluralism in Physics, Narratology, and Narrative,' *Poetics Today* 27(4): 633–674.

Index

www.ingramcontent.com/pod-product-compliance
Ingram Content Group UK Ltd.
Pitfield, Milton Keynes, MK11 3LW, UK
UKHW020409010325
455677UK00029B/820